Louise Prince

**THE GOLD AND SILVER
WYRE-DRAWERS**

H.R.H. Princess Alice Countess of Athlone, Honorary Freeman of the Company

THE GOLD & SILVER WYRE-DRAWERS

ELIZABETH GLOVER

PHILLIMORE

1979

Published by
PHILLIMORE & CO. LTD.,
London and Chichester

Head Office: Shopwyke Hall,
Chichester, Sussex, England

© Mrs. Elizabeth Glover, 1979

ISBN 0 85033 248 6

Typeset by COMPUTACOMP (UK) LTD.
Fort William, Scotland
Printed in Great Britain by
UNWIN BROTHERS LIMITED
at the Gresham Press, Old Woking, Surrey
and bound at
THE NEWDIGATE PRESS LTD.
Book House, Dorking, Surrey

Contents

	Introduction by H.R.H. Princess Alice Countess of Athlone	ix
	Foreword by the Master	xi
	Preface	xiii
1.	How Gold and Silver Wire was First Made and How it is Drawn Today	1
2.	What Happened before the First Charter	5
3.	How the Company Began	13
4.	How the Company and the Trade flourished in the 18th Century	22
5.	How the Trade and the Company changed in the 19th Century	31
6.	How the Trade changed in the 19th and 20th Centuries and how it is organised today	39
7.	What the Company is doing in the 20 Century	50
	Notes	63
	A list of those who have been Master	82
	A list of those who have been Clerk	85
	A list of those who have been Beadle	85
	Index	86

List of Illustrations

H.R.H. Princess Alice Countess of Athlone (*frontispiece*)

(between pages 34 and 35)

1. The practice of gold and silver wire-drawing today

2. Royal School of Needlework sampler

3. Exemplar presented by Bernard Thorpe

4. The first Charter

5. Nicholas Southouse

6. Beadle's mace head

7. Letterhead of Barrett & Corney

8. Letterhead of Benton & Johnson

9. Coat of Arms

10. Illuminated address presented to Herbert Toye

11. Sheriff's badge presented to Ralph Hedderwick

Bobbin label of Stephen Simpson   *page 49*

Introduction

As Honorary Freeman of the Worshipful Company of Gold and Silver Wyre Drawers, it gives me great pleasure to write these few words to introduce the new History of our Company. We have so much reason to be proud of the skills of the men and women employed in our craft over the centuries that it is right that we should be reminded of their problems and successes in what is intended to be a book that all can find of interest.

We are all aware of the elaborate service uniforms and regalia which have been largely based on our products, but it is also a special pleasure to me to know of the continued close association and support which our Company gives to the Royal School of Needlework, and the high standard of modern design and craftsmanship, which were admirably demonstrated at the Exhibition by the Company in Goldsmiths Hall in 1974. It is also a matter of satisfaction to me that the Company has recently adopted London Homes for the Elderly as the Charity which will have priority of interest in future.

It is important that we should continue to play our full part in the life of the City, and in the work of the trade as well as for the needs of charities, with which the Livery Companies have always been associated.

Alice Mary

Countess of Athlone

Foreword

>Market Buildings,
>29, Mincing Lane,
>London, E.C. 3.
>4th October, 1978

As Master this year of the Gold and Silver Wyre Drawers, I am, naturally, delighted that the history of the Company and the trade should be published now.

As history deals largely with the past, it is perhaps worth recording that new uses of gold and silver wire are always being found and I feel sure the Company will continue to flourish in the centuries ahead.

>R. C. A. FitzGerald

Preface

I am most grateful to Mr. Philip Cresswell C.C. for the help and information he has given me not only from his fund of personal knowledge of the Company but also for his interest in and erudite study of its history. My thanks are also due to Mr. David Reid F.C.A. and Mr. Norman Harding C.C. for information about the Company. Mr. Harding has also supplied information about the Company's Plate. For advice and much information on the trade I am indebted to Mr. J. F. Walmsley, Managing Director of Stephen Simpson (Northern Counties) Ltd., who also gave up a day to showing me round the works at Preston, to Mr. E. H. Leigh owner of G. L. Tootell and to Mr. E. C. Fitch, Managing Director of John Sharp (Gold Thread Ltd.). Mr. Dennis Johnson of Benton and Johnson has helped me greatly with information about the trade and the Company, as also has Mr. Roland Benton whose letters have been a delight. For information about the Royal School of Needlework and about embroidery my thanks are due to Mr. David Lloyd. I have been counselled and informed about the Arms by Mr. A. Colin Cole, T.D., B.C.L., M.A., F.S.A., Windsor Herald of Arms. The staff of the Guildhall Library have helped with books and topographical details. I have to thank Mr. Robert Horton not only for much information about the Company and the trade but also for his help and encouragement in the writing. I am indebted to Mr. Douglas Dunstan, Mr. Leslie Cork and Mr. Clifford Jeapes for their encouragement and stimulation. I have availed myself of the wise counsels of Mr. Sheriff Ralph Hedderwick C.C. The late Mrs. Eira Capstick and Mrs. Robin Wilkinson who have done the typing have been everlastingly patient, accurate and intelligent. Above all I must thank my husband for his exacting standards, and his unstinting and outspoken criticism.

Elizabeth Glover
Cock House, Langcliffe

I

How Gold and Silver Wire was First Made and How It is Drawn Today

PEOPLE HAVE been making gold and silver wire for a long time. The Egyptians[1] and the Babylonians[2] knew all about it before 2,000 B.C. and the Indians and the Chinese were probably proficient in the craft at an even earlier date.[3] The Bible describes the art[4] and Herodotus[5] and Apuleius[6] mention its existence. That long enduring saint, St. Eloi,[7] artisan and bishop who lived from c.588 to 660[8] is reputed to have been one of the earliest makers of gold and silver wire in Europe.[9]

The early gold and silver wire however was not drawn, it was made by gilding skins with gold foil. The vellum was then cut into very thin strips and wound round a thread of silk or hemp so closely that it looked like solid gold wire.[10] This method was the one the Venetians used during the Middle Ages and on into the mid-17th century.[11] More conservative buyers preferred wire made in this way and it was reputed to be less wasteful of the gold. This kind of wire is still occasionally made today and is sometimes used by the Royal School of Needlework for repairs.[12]

The art of drawing wire—that is, pulling the gold coated silver bar through a die set with ever smaller and smaller holes until the wire is produced—seems to have been first known in Germany at Augsburg and Nuremberg in the mid-14th century.[13] It was probably used there later on in the renowned armoury workshops.[14] The secret had spread to England at least as early as the late 1470's[15] and wire drawing was firmly established in London by the 1570's.[16]

The early process was the same in principle as the one used today, but of course the details have been constantly improved. In 1570 a Frenchman called Anthony Fournier is said to have brought the art of drawing wire exceedingly fine to Nuremburg.[17] Flatting wire—that is the process of flatting the wire so it can be wound round silk to make thread—was probably introduced at Augsburg in the mid-16th century.[18] The introduction of powered machinery in the 19th century greatly increased speed and accuracy.[19] The methods used were jealously guarded and it is difficult to be absolutely sure of the details of a craft which was not even revealed to contemporaries. Richard Babington who had bought the excise on gold silver and copper wire complained to the Commissioners for the Excise in 1655 that he was not getting a fair return on his investment of £2,000 because 'they erect engines [that is machines in modern English] in cellars and obscure places to disgross these goods without bringing them to the Commissioners of Excise'.[20]

The 17th-century shyness of competition and of the Excise has resulted in extreme obscurity for the historian. It therefore seems better to describe the modern methods as carried out at Stephen Simpson's works at Preston; the only now surviving firm to draw gold and silver wire in Britain; and then to indicate as accurately as possible how these methods vary from those used in the 17th century.

First, the quantities of silver of government specified quality are weighed. The specified quality is an alloy of $92\frac{1}{2}\%$ silver to $7\frac{1}{2}\%$ of copper which is the very same sterling standard as that laid down in the 12th century. The silver is then melted in a crucible to the correct molten heat. The charcoal hearth of the 17th-century craftsmen has been replaced by a gas-fired blow furnace, and the correct heat which the 17th century judged by eye is now officially decided by delicate and exact pyrometrical controls. The principle, however, is exactly the same, and having watched the process at Stephen Simpson's I have no doubt that Mr. Albert Redman, who now conducts this part of the operation, could easily dispense with the controls and that his eye and experience are as exact as those of his 17th-century predecessors. When the metal has reached the right heat it is poured into a chill casting mould set upright. After only a few moments the metal has solidified and the mould is laid on the furnace room floor. The clamps are released and the two halves of the mould are separated, leaving the metal in the form of a bar or 'billet'. The bar is then quenched and cooled in a water trough. This bar is in fact bottle shaped, and measures 27in. from the point of the shoulder to the bottom of the bottle or the 'sink' end. It is $2-2\frac{1}{2}$ins. in diameter and weighs about 550 ozs. troy. The tapered or 'point' end is made so that it is small enough to be held by the grapple tongs which are used when the bar comes to be drawn on the draw bench.

The bar is then put in a turning lathe where a cut of about $\frac{1}{16}$in. removes any surface faults. By this the bar is reduced to 2in diameter. The waste or swarf is carefully swept up and saved and goes back in the melting pot after refining. The finishing process begun in the lathe is then continued by hand and eye and of course in the 17th century it would all have been done by hand and eye. This is done at a shaving bench where the workman uses a two handled blade to cut away the pitholes, cracks and crevices, which are minor faults from casting and which show on the metal face.

The bar is then forged. It is annealed in a special furnace to give it the necessary malleability and is then placed under a power hammer. This hammer was originally driven by steam but is now powered by electricity. In the 17th century all this will have been done by hand, eye and sinew. It is not surprising that so many of the earlier gold and silver wire drawers obtained admission to the Blacksmiths' Company.[21] The purpose of the forging is to increase the tensile strength of the bar so it can be drawn. The forging increases the length to $31\frac{3}{4}$ins., i.e. by 25%, and decreases the diameter proportionately.

The first drawing then takes place. This is done by pulling the bar through a series of draw holes, each slightly smaller than the last, on a short draw bench. In the 19th century the bench was powered by steam; it is now powered by electricity. In the 17th century the tractile power will have been human or animal probably assisted by wheels and pulleys. It is here probably that one can understand such men as Philip Washborne (see Chapter III), when they did not wish to reveal the secrets of their workrooms to other wire drawers. A more ingenious arrangement of pulleys and wheels on their machines would obviously have given considerable increases in facility and speed and hence productivity to the inventor which he would naturally not wish to share with his competitors. Before declaring that 17th-century men were narrow minded it might be remembered that they were not protected by a Patents Act, and were engaged in a highly competitive trade requiring very heavy capitalisation.

When the bar has been drawn into a rod of 5ft. it is extensively cleaned in acids and its face polished. It is then ready for gilding. The proportion of gold to silver has still to meet government requirements which were until recently 2.5% gold to 88% silver, and 9.5% alloy. The new standards are 2.0% of gold to 1% silver and 97% white metal. The white metal is 90% copper, 5% nickle and 5% zinc. Times have indeed changed, but so has the material cost of specie.

The gold is applied in the form of gold foil which is laid on a gilding board. The gold foil is wrapped round the rod so as to cover it completely and equally. It is rolled to expel any air pockets. It is then put in a tubular burnishing oven to anneal. When it comes out of this oven it is a dull copper colour. It is then placed in a slowly rotating burnishing lathe where it is burnished with smooth stones. The men operating the process have to exert great pressure on the intensely hot rod which revolves a number of times. This process was carried out by hand in the 15th century using chalcedony stones. The rod at this stage is about $1^{1}/_{4}$ins. in diameter.

The rod then goes to the long draw bench devised by Isaac Simpson the younger, and passes through a series of many single holes until its original 5ft. becomes 100ft. The process is then continued by drawing it through other machines, ever lengthening and becoming finer, until the rod is no longer a rod but a length of wire. The 17th-century process was much the same but a series of benches had to be used. The principle of passing the metal through a mill or steel plate perforated with holes of different diameters was exactly the same.[22]

If fine wire is then required, the wire is nowadays passed at high speed through a series of diamond dies. The wire in common sizes in daily use can vary from 300 to 2,000 yards to the oz. troy. One cannot imagine that any such very fine wires were makeable before the use of powered machinery and indeed no examples have survived.

If the wire is required for making gold thread it is then flattened, a process hitherto undertaken by hand and which was Isaac Simpson's first essay in the industry.[23] Nowadays it is done by passing the wire at high speed through cambered rollers. In the 18th century the flattening was done as follows: two rollers were used, made of iron and welded over with a plate of refined steel. The rollers were cylindrical and carefully polished. They were placed with their axes parallel and their circumferences nearly in contact. Both rollers were turned by one handle. The lower was about 10 ins. in diameter, the upper about 2 ins. They were a little more than 1 in. in thickness. The wire was unwound from its bobbin and passed through the leaves of a book which was gently pressed and then through a narrow slit in an upright piece of wood called a ketch. It was then directed by a small conical hole in a piece of iron called a guide to any particular part of the width of the rollers. Some rollers took as many as 40 threads.[24]

The flattened wire is then spun onto silk or man-made fibre. In fact in many ways the man-made fibre is better since it does not rot, but the Royal Navy still maintains an ancient prejudice, embodied in many Acts of Parliament, against spinning gold and silver wire on to inkle or inferior thread and insists that only silk shall be used. The spinning is done by machine, one machine operating many spinning heads.

The wire used for this is drawn down to 1,500 yards to the oz. The Government specification for the Royal Navy is 480 yards to the oz. Troy or 7,000 yards per lb. avoir dupois. Early in the 17th century the spinners were using the chear and spindle alone for this process but had begun to use pedal wheels by the 1650's.[25] By the 1760's proper machines were being used.

The wire can also be woven straight into lace, some with a gold and silver wire weft and some with a gold and silver thread weft which is known as orris lace. This term orris lace is very old. These laces are woven on Jacquard looms and are supplied for uniform wear. They are sported by such divers people as the State Trumpeters of the Household Cavalry, the Guards bandsmen, the Royal Navy, the Merchant Navy, Hotel porters and Theatre attendants.

A further process turns the wire into numerous patterns for use in embroidery. These patterns are ancient and have enchanting names, purls, checks, bead, lizardine, pearl purl and spangles. The purls are made by winding the wire round a round needle to make a long curled spring. Checks are made by a similar process but using a triangular needle. Pearl purl is the beaded surround much used as a border for blazer badges. Spangles are small flat pieces, rather like sequins. The 17th century embroiderers would have had no difficulty in recognising these materials and neither the names nor the patterns have changed.[26]

Stephen Simpson also quite legitimately make an electroplated wire and a cheaper wire which is silver and gold laid on a copper core. The specifications of this wire are 2% gold on a base of 50% silver, 50% copper. A silver bar is cast and a hole bored in which a copper rod is inserted, the whole is then drawn and the final specification of the finished wire is quoted as 2% gold to 50% silver. This is used for cheaper quality embroidery materials today.[27] In the 17th century it was always being made but was illegal. In the 18th century it was only permitted for theatrical costumes. It is perhaps as well that Thomas Violet, who caused a man called Gares to stand in the pillory for just this practice,[28] should only be able to see these things from the shadows.

II

What Happened before the First Charter

TRADE IN Gold and Silver Wire with Britain started very early, probably by the 7th century, certainly by 1246 when the Cistercian Monks were using it in ecclesiastical embroidery.[1] It was well established by 1304 when a piece of gold and silk 'now weaving' was sold by Thomas Guy Dichon of Lucca to Alison Darcy.[2] When the Society of Antiquaries opened the tomb of Edward I in 1774, the body which had been buried in 1307 was found to be wrapped in a mantle of cloth of gold.[3] There is the even earlier instance of St. Cuthbert, who was wearing a tunicle and dalmatic, the borders stiff with gold thread when exhumed in 1104,[4] but it is possible that this was exceptional, especially in view of the amazement expressed by Simeon of Durham who describes the exhumation. Indeed, it cannot even be assumed that the clothes worn by the body are those in which it was originally buried in 687, for we know from Bede that St. Cuthbert was dug up and undressed at least once.[5]

English embroidery with its plentiful use of gold and silver wire and semi-precious stones was renowned in the 13th century, and the London workshops ran a profitable export trade. The Vatican inventory of 1295 lists more examples of what it called Opus Anglicanum, that is English work, than any other kind of embroidery. Many of the best surviving pieces are still to be found in European churches and museums. Most of this work was financed by London merchants and carried out in workshops by masters of the craft, among them Rose de Burford who made a cope for Isabella, the faithless wife of Edward II, in 1317. As time went on this work called ever more heavily on gold and silver wire and the backgrounds to the embroideries were heavily worked in gold. The Marnhull orphrey made between 1315 and 1335 positively shimmers with elaborate heraldic devices worked in gold wire.[6]

The trade grew steadily in the later Middle Ages. An Act of 2 Richard II (1378/79) gave permission to foreign merchants to reside in England and trade in gold and silver wire.[7] The privy purse expenses of Elizabeth of York in 1502 mention the purchase of flat and round gold from the Queen's broderer.[8] The nobility, not only the Royal family and ecclesiastics, began to patronise the trade; Sir John Howard bought a long cloak of cloth of gold lined with damask in 1462.[9]

Acts of Parliament obtained by the Wardens and Fellowship of Broderers' in 1423 against the making of silver and gold with copper for embroidery and in 1489 against the deceitful weight and working of gold of Venice, Florence and Genoa, and the untrue packing thereof,[10] show the City of London's early association with the Trade and its rightful preoccupation with standards.

As elaborateness and display in dress increased so did the trade. Henry VIII's extravaganza at the Field of the Cloth of Gold was indeed a field day for gold and silver wire drawers.[11] Even the Tree of Honour which supported the shields of the challengers at the elaborate tournament which was part of the so-called diplomatic mission was made of much 'Venice' gold.[12] Edward VI had a jerkin embroidered with 'Venice' silver[13] and the fringe on his funeral furniture was made of Venice gold.[14] Ladies began buying the materials so they might embroider for themselves. In 1523 Dame Agnes Hungerford owned a casket which contained various types of silver gilt thread including Venice gold and damask gold and silks for embroidery.[15] In 1597 Lady Katherine Petre apprenticed Margaret Davis, a member of her household, to Josine Graunger, a London embroideress, to learn how to work among other things gold and silver.[16]

Much of this wire, however, was of foreign manufacture. In 1511 and 1513 Francis de Barde, a merchant of Florence, Lawrence Bonnixi of Lucca and William Bull a mercer of London were granted licences to import cloth of gold.[17] As late as 1577 Sir John Petre, Margaret's father-in-law, was buying Venice gold for upholstery work.[18] Until well into the next century Venice gold and silver wire was thought to be of better quality.

Gold and silver wire was being made in England however and by the new process of drawing, at least as early as 1476. In that year John Framlyngham acknowledged a deed of gift to William Hody, John Wydeslade and Christopher Hanyngton gentlemen; of divers tools, irons and instruments belonging to the craft of working of wire called gold wire drawing. These tools were: six great irons, 13 small irons [I assume these were the draw plates], three stocks with three anvils set in them to make flat gold, four whetstones, two chalcedony stones, two hammers, two files, two anvils, four hammers, three pincers, six pairs of tongs, three pairs of bellows, six stools to work on, two pairs of balances, two candlesticks, 16 great rollers and 12 small, six files and a wheel, two chests, two rolls to roll upon flat gold, three ingots with other small things, such as nippers and pointels, boxes and a stamp. Stephen Simpson's complete equipment, in fact. A little primitive perhaps but perfectly adequate. What is fascinating also about this gift is that it was part of a marriage settlement between John and his wife, Anne. Anne was to rule and guide the said instruments and occupation and 'all things concerning the same and take and perceyve [*sic*; ? receive] all manner [of] profits'. If Anne were prevented by her husband from exercising the craft then William, John and Christopher were to depute someone in her stead to carry on the trade for her benefit.[19] It seems likely that the wire drawing business was Anne's own, inherited from either a previous husband or her father. How delightful that the first English wiredrawer we know by name should have been a woman and, as we shall see later, how appropriate.

There is further evidence of the English practice of the craft in the Wardrobe Accounts. The lists for 1536–7 and 1547 include payments to a wiredrawer, not a merchant, for pipes and purls for a gown for my Lady's Grace.[20]

Certainly the art was well known and frequently practised by the 1570's. The Commissions of Oyer and Terminer held in 1620 established this with the evidence of a very old man called Herrenden who told them that he had made gold and silver wire for above fifty years.[21] The household accounts of Sir John Petre show he patronised two London wire-drawers in the 1570's. They were called Edward Burchall and Thomas Hall, and both lived in Crooked Lane.[22] Another witness to the 1620 commissions, one Mary Forest, gave evidence that she had been apprenticed in 1596 at the age of 10 to a Frenchman called John Rosineall who made thread and taught her and others.[23] This would of course accord with the known Elizabethan policy of offering sanctuary to persecuted protestants abroad as well for the skills which they brought into the country as for more direct political reasons.

What is known about the organisation of the trade is very interesting. The number of master craftsmen seems to have been small; one contemporary, Thomas Violet, puts it at thirty.[24] These seem to have been men trained originally in the more ancient crafts of the Broderers, the Mercers and the Goldsmiths.[25] The master craftsmen, however, controlled large numbers of outworkers, mostly women and children. Mary Forest immediately springs to mind as an early example. An early 18th-century petition says they were seamen's widows and numbers them at 20,000, but this was propaganda. The particular functions of the outworkers are listed in the same petition as follows: wire-drawers, flatters, spinners, twisters, lace weavers, bone lace makers, embroiderers, flourishers of muslin, button makers, fancy ribbon weavers, broad weavers, the makers of tissues, brocades and other rich flowered silks and stuffs.[26]

Naturally such a situation of male dominance and female dependence led to charges of exploitation. Violet, who did not like the master wiredrawers and complained that they were people of several humours and some of uncivil and coarse behaviour, was particularly poetic in expressing them.[27] He describes work-people who 'with tears in their eyes' told him they were forced to work the masters' coarse and deceitful silver wire and thread contrary to their consent, to get bread.[28] This is too much in tune with the normal reaction of any employee charged by a bureaucrat to be acceptable as evidence of real exploitation. In fact the masters and their outworkers were, as today, inter-dependent and certainly the workers were not exploited financially. The 18th-century petition gives the wages as 18d. to 20d. per week and to 2s. to 2s. 6d. per week for bone lace makers;[29] this, when bread cost 4d. for a 4lb. loaf, beef and mutton were 3d. a lb. and cheese $2\frac{1}{2}$d. a lb.,[30] was not low pay for secondary outworkers and was rather more than other textile workers were earning.

One set of outworkers however do seem to have been convinced of a genuine grievance. These were the workers with chear and spindle on the thread spinning side. The introduction of the spinning wheel was obviously a threat to their livelihood and they contested with the usual plea that the faster work was more wasteful. They said that the handspinner's work was necessary for embroidery and the making of fringes, and would return 2s. 8d. to the ounce when melted. The wheel work would only return 1s. 6d.[31]

There were certainly abuses of other kinds. English gold and silver wire and thread was not of the quality of the Venice manufacture. The Venice weights were 6 oz. of silver to 2 oz. of silk to make a lb. Venice, whereas the English weights were often as light as 3 oz. of silver and 5 oz. of silk to a lb. Venice or in extreme cases 4 oz. of coarse silver and 4 oz. of heavy dyed silk to a lb. Venice.[32] The Venice gold and silver thread was also made in skeins and could all be returned to the melting pot, whereas the English was wasted and the bullion was not good.[33] In addition, there were many complaints about the practice of plating silver with gold on a copper core or annealing silver on a copper core (this is incidentally a practice quite acceptable today.) The complaints of the Broderers' in 1423[34] and of Richard Babington in 1655[35] are both about this practice. Violet in his work as Master of the Assay of Gold and Silver Wire in the late 1630's came across an interesting case of this fraud in which many people, some of them very respectable, were involved. He discovered on his own account 50lbs. of silver lace mixed with copper in no less a person's house than the Lord Mayor of London, Alderman Garroway. He confiscated this as he was entitled to do, but it was not until later that he discovered a further fraud; the enterprising merchants had not only been cheating the home market but had actually been exporting to Russia. Unfortunately the Czar's council discovered the fraud and actually imprisoned Sir Thomas Sandys, Alderman Garroway's brother-in-law, who had brought the lace into the country. Sir Thomas appears to have been innocently duped and when the Czar had confirmed this the Muscovy company were asked to investigate. The result of their investigation proved the point and 20 men, rather than wait to be accused, ran away.[36]

The trade was of course a luxury one, Monarchs and Courtiers were the biggest buyers. Not all purchases, however, can have been so pathetic as Charles I's. Between 27th December 1648 and 3rd January 1649, that is 27 days before his execution, he bought three new suits, two of them cloth with rich gold and silver lace on them.[37] Other purchases were more amusing. Henry VIII bought a pair of stockings of purple silk and Venice gold woven like a caul.[38] A less well known person, although a man of considerable eminence in the county of Essex, Sir John Petre, had a pair of purple velvet hose embroidered with silver and drawn out of cloth of silver.[39] The City Companies and the Corporation also patronised the trade. The Girdlers' Company, for example, have listed in their book of benefactors a Master's Crown made of gold and silver wire and thread which they still have in their possession.[40] The Vintners' Company were given a hearse cloth of cloth of gold and velvet and a corporas of gold by the Chamberlain of London, John Hussey, in 1539 and still display the hearse cloth at their Hall.[41] The Corporation of London's city purse is made of gold and silver wire.[42]

It is difficult to set prices in context because of the differences in relative values and because of the rapid inflation of our own times. Henry VIII paid £7 17s. 0d. for the pipes and purls for the gown of my Lady's Grace.[43] Sir John Petre paid 14s. in 1577 for an oz. of Venice gold and an oz. of silver.[44] His embroidered stockings cost 25s. in 1581.[45] Two yards of cloth of silver for his lady cost £6 3s. 9d.[46] Although the Government, fighting inflation in those days, on its own behalf as well as the country's, issued an order in Council in 1581 directing shopkeepers to reduce by one quarter the price of gold cloth, so that ladies and gentlemen might be better able to bedizen themselves for the visit of the French Marriage Embassy, prices still rose. Cloth of silver which had been 19s. a yard in 1577 rose to 55s. in 1581.[47] In the late 17th century a knotted fringe belt for the Earl of Bedford cost £5, a silver embroidered hat £5 10s. 0d., and broad gold wire £3 13s. 0d. the yard.[48] These prices may seem more immediate if set against the following prices: in the Tudor period, bread was 1d. a loaf, beer 1d. for $^2/_3$rds of a gallon, and 2 lbs. of beef cost 3d.[49] A workman could buy a yard of the cheapest cloth for one day's wage. His wages for the half year would hardly buy a yard of the dearest and a fine cloak at £20 would require three years labour.[50]

The gold and silver trimmings, buttons, thread and fringes accounted, even where prices of cloth were high, for the greater part of the cost of clothes.[51]

Even so the trade was obviously flourishing and the reasons for this were closely connected with the economic factors of the period. The Tudors and Stuarts, as we do, lived in a period of rapid inflation. S. T. Bindoff calculates that prices had doubled within two years of the death of Henry VIII in 1547[52] and Professor Tawney estimates that James I had inherited a rise in prices of approximately 50% between Elizabeth's accession in 1558 and his own accession in 1603.[53] The inflation was particularly beneficial to the cloth trade, of which gold and silver wire drawing was a part. S. T. Bindoff estimates that the trade in short cloths through London doubled in Henry VIII's reign alone.[54] It was also particularly advantageous to new industries such as gold and silver wire drawing because it made capital more easily available. The market was also expanding because new men were coming to power, and spending money on elaborate clothes, a thing not much approved of by contemporaries such as Philip Stubbes who animadverted viciously upon the changes in society and the extravagances of the rising class. He said: 'It is very hard to know who is noble and who is worshipful, who is a gentleman and who is not for you shall have those who go daily in silks, velvets, satins, damasks, taffaties and such like notwithstanding that they be both base by birth, mean by estate and servile by calling'.[55]

Unfortunately inflation had other effects not so beneficial to the trade and these effects were further complicated by the economic theories and constitutional complications of the day. It is well known that those most affected by inflation are those with fixed incomes. Unfortunately at that period this included the Government of the day, that is, the Crown. Henry VIII, by his confiscation of the monastery lands, contrived to modify the effects of this on himself and to some extent on his descendants, and Elizabeth's shrewd financial policies helped to prolong the process but towards the end of her reign she was driven to expedients which were unpopular with Parliament. This was especially so of the granting of monopolies. The Stuarts continued this policy when they became more in need of money as their relations with Parliament grew worse.

Parliament was against the granting of monopolies not only on principle as an obnoxious practice but also because it helped to make it possible for the Crown to govern without Parliament. The Commission of Oyer and Terminer in 1620, already referred to, was called because of a complaint by the Commons against the grant of a monopoly for gold and silver wire.[56] Although the King gave way because he wanted a grant from Parliament, he did not stop the practice, and monopolies were granted and rescinded throughout the Stuart period. Parliament made its final complaint against them in the Grand Remonstrance.[57]

It is difficult to say whether in fact the craft benefited or suffered from these monopolies. There is certainly an argument for granting monopolies to new and struggling industries, but the Crown seems to have been more interested in the money it could acquire and the courtiers it could reward than in the industry itself. Fowle's patent was called in question in 1624 because 'his wire is of less value and of higher price than imported and consumes much bullion';[58] not a recommendation. Meanwhile the King had been paid a sum equal to that obtained from the duty on importation, and Sir Edward Villiers, one of the Council, had also an 'interest' in the matter.[59] Thomas Violet on the other hand, when appointed Master of the Assay for gold and silver wire in the late 1630's, seems to have made real efforts to improve the standards. The King however did not stand to lose—he had been paid £1,500 for the concession.[60]

Unfortunately for the trade both Parliament and the Crown had other reasons for attacking the art of gold and silver wire drawing. This attack was of a more formidable kind, and the reasons for it were based on the respectable economic theories of the day. The economy was then thought to be based on the value of gold and silver, and from this naturally followed the idea that a good balance of trade would keep gold and silver in the country and not waste them on goods which would be sent abroad, or from which bullion would be lost while in the country. The use of gold and silver wire was disliked because there was some loss during manufacture and some loss in wear. In 1617–18 several royal proclamations were made prohibiting the manufacture of gold and silver thread and restricting the use of gold leaf.[61] The House of Commons complained about this aspect of affairs in 1620[62] and when Violet was granted the assay he was particularly charged with maintaining standards which would preserve bullion.[63] Against the background of the Crown's anxiety about money, the balance of trade, and its constitutional difficulties with Parliament, enters a character who has been mentioned already in these pages, Thomas Violet.

Thomas Violet was an ingenious and ingenuous man of obscure origins. One pamphlet accuses him of being of mixed Dutch and Moorish blood and of being born on board ship.[64] He first came to James I's notice when Sir Edward Coke, then Secretary to the Privy Council, discovered that he had been playing the money market by exchanging English silver coin for French gold. Violet seems to have been surprised at being discovered and remarks in one of his pamphlets: 'When I saw it [i.e. Sir Edward's evidence] I was astonished not imagining that anyone did know my proceedings in the business or that I was betrayed by those that spake me fair'.[65] He was put in prison but bought himself out by showing that the exchanges had been to his benefit, (Coke made him produce his books) and therefore to the country's. He also paid a fine of £2,000 to the Privy Purse.[66] According to Violet this was because 'King James had admired his [Violet's] ingenuity but thought he should share in the profits'.[67]

Violet and the Crown having thus become acquainted, Charles I found use for him by giving him the survey of all gold and silver wire making. For this Violet paid £1,500.[68] Incidentally it was because of this grant that the attempts to form an incorporated livery company, which will be discussed in Chapter III, were frustrated. Violet seems, at any event by his own account, to have made efforts to place the manufacture on a reputable footing with standards as high as those of the Venetian work, a task for which he was well fitted having engaged in malversation even while he was an apprentice. On his own evidence he delivered £20,000 of heavy shillings and sixpences to Alderman Gibbs for his master during one year to be melted into ingots and to be used for manufacture.[69]

During his holding of the assay he instituted a special system for sealing the skeins with the assay mark of a Rose and Crown on one end, and the craftsmen's mark on the other.[70] He also caused a man called Gares to stand in the pillory for making gold and silver thread with a core of copper and even had the temerity to question Master Bradbourn, 'the Queen's silkman' of all people, for putting copper into an honourable lady's silver lace and into Lord Carlisle's suit and cloak. Who knows to what lengths he might have gone if the Queen had not happened to intervene? He of course obliged her by dropping further proceedings.[71]

Violet fell foul of Parliament during the Civil War and was sent to the Tower in 1643 but he had only himself to blame. He ingenuously approached Parliament with a petition from the King and being on the wanted list himself he was immediately committed.[72] He managed somehow to 'procure' his release and after the King's death, with happy bravado, put his services at the disposal of the Lord Protector, Cromwell. He also petitioned for a regrant of his office of assay, but the whole process of granting monopolies had been too severely criticised by the Long Parliament for this to be allowed.[73]

At the Restoration, Violet was loud in his protestations of loyalty and recitations of his services to the late King but although he regained his post at the Mint[74] (an office he had also managed to acquire), he was never re-instated in the assay of gold and silver wire. He thus ceased to be connected directly with the trade, but in view of the subsequent history of the Company, which was soon to be incorporated, it may be of interest to note that Violet certainly had dealings and connections with the Jews and that he wrote a particularly virulent pamphlet against them.[75] Probably, in all justice let it be said, in self defence rather than from conviction.

The Restoration produced one odd piece of legislation which has some bearing on the history of the Trade. This was an Act of 1678 which forbade the wearing of any shrouds or grave clothes except those of wool. Interestingly enough the Act specifies as unacceptable alternatives 'those made of or mingled with Flax, Silk, Hemp, Gold or Silver'.[76] The effect of this Act could only be marginal on the trade and in practice many people of substance preferred to pay the fine rather than wear anything so 'odious' as wool, and gold and silver continued to be used in grave clothes. In 1747 the Parish Clerk of Bromley, Kent, dug up a crown or garland buried in the grave of a young girl which was artificially wrought in 'filigree' work of gold and silver wire to resemble myrtle and which was 'lined with cloth of silver'.[77]

By the end of the 1670's the manufacture of gold and silver wire was established in England. The trade, if the expenses of the Earl of Bedford at Charles II's Coronation are any indication, was flourishing. The Earl paid £120 to the gold and silver workers for the embroidery fringes and other trimmings for his suit and that of his son William.[78]

The craft had even entered the literature of that golden age and the image of gold wire had been used by Shakespeare,[79] Spenser[80] and Milton.[81] The Constitutional conflict between Parliament and the Crown which had produced political difficulties was to be over by 1688 and matters were set fair for the incorporation of the present Company.

III

How the Company Began

THE COMPANY was granted a full Charter of Incorporation on 16th June 1693.
Unlike it's abortive predecessor in 1623[1] (see below) this charter was a common form document very much like that of any other City Company and could not have been more constitutional and proper. It had passed through all the regular procedures. A petition was made to the Attorney General 1691[2] who referred it to the Court of Aldermen in March, the Court of Aldermen referred it to a Committee who delivered a report in its favour in the same month.[3] The Aldermen then instructed the City solicitor John Borrett who was to become the Company's first clerk to proceed with the matter, only adding the proviso that: the Company should not be therefore enabled to take any members though of the same trade from any of the Companies already established without first obtaining the licence and approbation of their Court.[4] The draft was then perused by the Recorder and the Charter was granted in 1693, and enrolled in the Records of the City in September of the same year.[5]

By the Charter the Company became a corporate body with full legal status, so that it could sue and be sued, hold land, have a common seal and generally conduct its own affairs. The ruling body was to be a Master and four Wardens with an original Court of 24 Assistants which with the passing of time might extend to 36 but not beyond. Thirteen, of whom the Master or one of the Wardens must be one, was to constitute a quorum. The Master was named as Nathaniel Smith, citizen and gold and silver wire drawer, the Wardens as Henry Scatcliffe, Thomas Wright, Jacob Sheldrake and Richard Andrews. The Assistants were William Newbery, Peter Floyer, Thomas Woods, Thomas Jett, Zachary Hickcox, Thomas Bracce, Henry Southhouse, Robert Rhodes, Joseph Tucker, William Wastfield, Francis Smartfoot, William Cousens, John Field, Robert Rouse, Christopher Blower, Joseph Horsley, Job Harris, Samuel Parratt, John Fisher, Samuel Harridge, William Swift, Daniel Biddle, Henry Lovelace and Daniel Field. The date of election for the Master was to be 30th December and elections were to be held yearly to appoint the Master and Wardens. The Court was to appoint a Clerk and a Beadle and oaths were laid down which were to be taken by the Officers and by the Master, Wardens and Court. In addition, the Company was to have the right to oversee and make rules for the 'goodness' of all sorts of gold and silver thread and for the 'goodness' of spinning of brass and copper and other inferior metals. To enforce this the Company was given rights of search and confiscation under Warrant of the Lord Chief Justice of the King's bench and the right to inspect all weights and measures used in the industry provided this did not conflict with the Goldsmiths' more ancient right to try all weights beams and scales. The right of search was to extend to London and within thirty miles of it. The Company was also to have the right to enforce membership, oversee apprentices, and supervise those outworkers who because of their sex or age were not eligible for the freedom.[6]

This charter represented a great triumph for the members of the Company who had negotiated it. One has only to compare it with the earlier abortive charter of 1623. The 1623 charter was issued in very odd circumstances. It had been granted in typical Stuart fashion immediately after the King's proclamation of 1622 forbidding the manufacture of gold and silver thread altogether. It was a compact of a most dubious kind which not only defeated parliamentary claims for interference in monetary affairs but also undermined the ancient and constitutional powers of the City. The rule was placed not in the hands of a Master who was to be elected yearly but in that of a Governor who was to hold the office for life. This Governor was appointed by the King and was none other than Matthias Fowle of Violet fame (see Chapter II). In addition to this he could be removed, not as was usual by the action of the Company through the Court of Aldermen, but at the pleasure of the King on the complaint of six or more of the members of the Privy Council. The supervisory powers given to the Company were to be subject to the control of the Assay Master of the Mint, a Royal Appointment, as well as that of the Assay Master of the Goldsmiths' Company, a city appointment. The prosecution of offenders was not to be through the Court of Aldermen but through the Attorney General in the Kings prerogative Court of Star Chamber. As if the Star Chamber were not ill-omened enough, add to this that Francis Garroway of the Russian export swindle was mentioned as one of the proposed freemen of the Company and it is not surprising that the affair was scandalous to contemporaries.[7] However it came to nothing as the King felt he could do better by appointing Violet Assay Master instead.

In addition to the early contests with the Crown the Gold and Silver Wire Drawers had to overcome some city opposition. After the Restoration the gold and silver wire-drawers had campaigned vigorously for a Charter[8] but had been opposed by the Goldsmiths' Company who were concerned to protect their ancient privileges, and said that they felt confident that they could regulate the trade. Considering the history of the previous 60 years this seems optimistic to say the least and the Goldsmiths themselves, however confident, were willing to concede it to be so. A compromise was reached, which can still be seen in the Charter. Indeed the draft proposals as amended by the Goldsmiths became the basis of the Charter as finally granted.[9]

Triumph or not there remains the question of why the men who so campaigned thought it worth while, not only to go to so much trouble but also to spend the then very considerable sum of over six hundred pounds[10] out of their own pockets.[11] The more ancient city companies such as the Vintners' and the Salters' were already becoming disassociated from their trades and giving up their duties of search and with historical hindsight we know that these matters were to pass in future to the control of Parliament. The answer to some of this lies in the earlier history of the trade. The manufacture in England was of comparatively recent date and whereas the Wine trade and the Salt trade were established and not in need of protection the Gold and Silver Wire industry still needed control and respectability. The Gold and Silver Wyre Drawers were not alone in being granted a charter at this time; the Glass Sellers, another recent trade in need of organisation and protection, obtained their charter in 1664.[12] There is, too, the point that whereas looking back on history we can see that the old City system of control was failing and was to become archaic, to people living at the time the old methods and institutions were the normal methods of practice and the old formulae were the obvious ones to use. They were constitutional, respectable and acceptable.

The history of the two previous reigns had more than proved that the King's control of the trade was ineffectual and mercenary. Charles II alas proved no more reliable than his father and grandfather. In 1662/3 the Maids of Honour and the Mother of the King (Queen Henrietta Maria) petitioned Charles II to grant to trustees named by them a patent similar to the one conferred in the late reign on account of the corruption of Gold and Silver lace.[13] This was obviously an outrageous scheme for increasing the Queen's income unknown to Parliament and had no concern for the trade at all. It was so politically dangerous that the Attorney General turned it down out of hand.

A petition by John Garill in the same year was more favourably received.[14] On the face of it Garill was a much more respectable applicant. He was a gold and silver wire-drawer himself and a sufficiently well-known one to be asked to give evidence to the Goldsmiths' Company about the quality of wire made and assayed by the Gold and Silver wire-drawers when they were negotiating with the Goldsmiths in 1664.[15] Moreover Garill made his claim on the grounds that he had a new process 'for casting and preparing gold and silver ingots for making wire and lace'. The Attorney General approved. The Lord Treasurer approved. Sir Philip Warwick was informed by persons able to judge that 'Mr Garill's new mode of making gold and silver wire was both beautiful and durable and would save one ounce in twelve'. The anonymous persons so 'able to judge' advised that a patent should be granted if the invention was new. A warrant was issued on 3rd December 1663 and the patent was confirmed on 29th of the same month. This gave Garill the sole right of preparing gold and silver ingots to be drawn into gold and silver lace and the liberty to import gold and silver to do so. The other gold and silver wire-drawers thus found themselves in a very vulnerable position. Their protests were soon heard. An angry meeting was held at the house of Simon Urlin in Gutter Lane. Tempers were high and Urlin went so far as to say that the granting of patents was the cause of the late King's head being cut off. This was a highly treasonable statement which was immediately reported to the Privy Council. Charles II, perhaps wary of Urlin's warning, certainly with more good sense than his father would have shown, took no action.[16] Meanwhile the trade was still disorganised and vulnerable. The only obvious action was to obtain a regular charter and stop the Crown's periodic attempts to solve its financial difficulties.

The Charter itself provides two interesting pieces of information. It shows the extent of the trade and its reliance on women and children as outworkers. The powers of search, which in charters granted to other City Companies were confined to London and its suburbs, in this Charter extend to 30 miles round the metropolis. Provision is taken also for the women and children who have been employed in one particular branch or way of spinning gold and silver thread known by the name of hand-spinning, who are in no way capable of being received into the City of London or of the said corporation. These persons are still to be allowed employment and are to be subject to the ordinances of the Court, whether members of the Company or not, or whether married or not.[17]

As it happened, the women in the craft were treated most honourably from the first. Not only could widows become free of the Company on their husband's death,[18] which was quite a usual beneficent City concession—for example, it was a privilege granted to the widows of members of the Vintners' Company to allow them to carry on their husbands' businesses—but they could also become free by apprenticeship, which was unusual[19] and by patrimony which was exceptional.[20] The only two kinds of women who could not take up the freedom were those who were already married to men already free of the City[21] and those who remarried having been admitted as the widows of freemen.[22] Indeed the Company's attitude seems to have been the reverse of misogynistic. When women first began to be employed as engine spinners the Company was very determined that they should take up the freedom. As will be seen in Chapter IV, they did not resist the demand.[23]

To begin with the Company had to face all kinds of anomalies, not the least, that created by the question of the working wire drawers. The representatives of these men were named in the Court book as: Thomas Pensome, Philip Washborne, Edward Turner, Samuel Farrow, John Cheshire, John Smart, Samuel Smith, John Day, Richard Croom and Thomas Benson. Their demands were: that there should be an equal number of working wire drawers on the Court with the stuff makers, that there should not be too many apprentices, that the apprentices should serve eight years, that no freeman should take an apprentice until he had been free for four years, that no freeman should be able to take another apprentice until his first apprentice had served four years, that no apprentice should be turned over (that is, transferred from one master to another); that no apprentice should be left unbound for more than two months, that no one should be taught the trade who was not an apprentice and that prices (i.e. wages) should be increased to the workmen.[24]

This was in fact an excellent example of Trades' Union lobbying for increased wages and restrictive practices, but some of these ideas were ones with which the Company itself was largely in sympathy. The Company was equally interested in restrictive practices and indeed in some sense was set up to protect them. Even in the matter of the claim for an equal number of wire drawers on the Court it was prepared to make some concession and offered four places on the Court to the wire drawers.[25] Unfortunately the wire drawers were not prepared to accept this as sufficient[26] and retired in some dudgeon. Until compelled by the Court's appeal to the Court of Aldermen, they refused to become members of the Company.[27] The ill feeling shown by the working wire-drawers suggests that the men who petitioned, organised and paid for the charter and constituted the early Court were in the majority, the stuff makers. They were only too likely to have been because they represented the richer and more powerful side of the trade.

At first there seem to have been difficulties about apprenticeships, because although there were practising members of the craft not many of them had yet been made members of the Company. Some indeed took some persuading to join. Robert Darley, for example, not only refused to take up the freedom but was 'unbecoming in speech and behaviour.'[28] To overcome the difficulty about apprentices, the Company in its early days bound its apprentices to the Beadle who then turned them over to their real masters.[29] There were difficulties, too, about which people it was proper to admit and which not. In 1702 the question arose whether lace men and copper wire drawers might be admitted.[30]

It is interesting to see from what Companies the early membership was taken. Some trades were obviously allied and need no explanation and indeed these are the most numerous: Haberdashers,[31] Merchant Taylors,[32] Cordwainers,[33] Weavers,[34] Mercers,[35] Hat band makers,[36] Cloth workers,[37] Broderers,[38] Glovers,[39] from the stuff making side; Blacksmiths,[40] Armourers,[41] Goldsmiths,[42] Long Bow stringmakers[43] from the wire drawing end. The inclusion of Vintners,[44] Grocers,[45] Fishmongers,[46] Scriveners[47] and Salters[48] among these early wire drawers shows the already great disconnection of those companies with their ancient trades, and also demonstrates the growth and extent of the wire drawing craft.

The Company became an extremely effective body very rapidly. The Byelaws which were drawn up by the Court, and skilfully manoeuvred through their various necessary stages by that same John Borrett, the clerk of the company, who had negotiated the charter, received the approbation which was required by the Act of 25 January Henry VII (1503/4), of the Lord Chancellor, the Lord High Treasurer, and the Chief Justices of the King's Bench and of the Common Pleas on 17 October 1700.[49] These Byelaws constitute a document of common form after the regular manner of all City Companies. They lay down the date of the election of the Master, the Wardens, the Clerk and the Beadle, the fines and fees to be imposed, the dates of meeting, the dress to be adopted by the livery, if a livery is granted. They lay down that stewards shall be elected who shall provide dinners at certain specified times and that members shall not quarrel or combine or make conspiracies. The most interesting clauses relate to the measures for the regulation of the trade and what is especially interesting is that the Byelaws, as finally constituted, fulfil some of the demands of the working wire drawers. They include the provision that no freeman is to take an apprentice unless he himself is of two years standing, and he can only take a second after the first has served for three and a half years. Apprenticeships were to be for seven years not eight, but this after all was very much in tune with common city form.

The following provisions were made for controlling the trade. A stated size for wire by rings, and wire, was to be kept at the Hall of the Company, with a fee of 6d. for using it. This fee was to be paid by the workman if the wire was wrong, or by the Master if the wire was right. No gold or silver plate was to be spun on thread or inkle (a kind of linen tape or the thread or yarn from which it is made), as opposed to silk, and no gold or silver plate was to be spun otherwise than close, except frost (a kind of gold and silver thread used for embroidery) on different coloured silk or upon heavy dyed silk of either white or gold colour or on undyed silk. The fines were to be £5 for every pound of copper, brass or other inferior metal spun on silk, or of gold and silver plate spun on thread, or inkle or gold and silver spun on heavy dyed silk of white or gold or undyed silk. These Byelaws were no empty formulae; the Court immediately set about enforcing them by organising searches and by prosecuting the offenders. Indeed, the Company was so energetic in carrying out its duties that in 1701 the Court consulted the Attorney General about the extent of the privilege. He gave it as his opinion that the Company might search for defective gold and silver wire all over England.[50]

Some of those searched, like one Samuel Bennet, a spinner, were compliant. He confessed most engagingly that he had not spun close.[51] Some like Newton, another spinner, at least accepted his punishment and the searchers destroyed 1 oz. 1d. wt. of his silver thread because it was not of sufficient quality.[52] Phillip Washborne, who had already had some negotiations with the Company as a representative of the working wire drawers, showed a less tractable attitude and resisted both the search and the arrest.[53] His reasons for doing so were interesting, however, and he himself seems to have been a man of capacity and ingenuity. He obviously had no particular objection to the existence of the Company as such, since as early as 1693 he was prepared to take an apprentice under the Company's aegis,[54] but he resisted the search. He did this on the grounds that he might lose the secrets of his trade to other wire-drawers on the Court, and specifically asked that those members of the Court who used engines should not be allowed into his workroom.[55] This being agreed he submitted, and his reconciliation with the Company must eventually have been complete, for his son became Master in 1728. It is pleasant to know that the working wire drawers in at least one instance gained their demands for representation.

The Company also undertook the normal city duties of City Companies at this time. It made the usual contribution to the City's grain supply[56] which was raised so that in times of shortage the price of bread might be stabilised. It also contributed the statutory half crown for every apprentice enrolled towards the orphans' fund, which was established in 1694 for the support of city orphans.[57] Insofar as funds permitted it was generous to its own members. John Horsly had his donation of £3 towards the Charter refunded when he fell on hard times.

In other ways, too, the Court undertook its duties seriously, particularly in lobbying Parliament[58] in the interests of the trade. In January 1697/8 the Court resolved itself into a grand committee to attend the affairs of Parliament and to discuss with Sir Henry Hobart M.P. the Bill for restricting imports of foreign bone lace, loom lace, needlework, point cut work and gold and silver thread.[59] Throughout the year the Committee gave detailed consideration to the bill, finally deciding on the matters it considered most important. These were: that none should make gold and silver thread unless he had been apprenticed to a gold and silver wire drawer for seven years and was free of the Gold and Silver Wyre Drawers; that the Gold and Silver Wyre-Drawers Company should have the right of search throughout the kingdom; that gold and silver plate should be put on silk only; that no gilt wire should be coloured with verdigris; that no silver plate should be put on heavy dyed silk; that no copper or brass should be spun on inkle.[60] The Company's demands were obviously rather large and it seems also to have had some kind of dispute with Sir Henry Hobart, for later in the same year the Company asked Sir Robert Davers to help it instead.[61]

Not all the Company's demands were met. The Bill on passing the Commons made no mention of the Company's rights and was exact in the quality of silver wire to be drawn for silver thread, a matter which the Committee had either not considered important or had thought controversial. The level of quality fixed is very interesting in that it was to be at least 11 oz. 16d. wt. of fine silver on every pound weight, all silver gilt to be of the same quality. This is only just below Violet's estimate of the quality of Venice Gold and Silver wire which was 12 oz. to every pound weight. In the gilding not less that 4d. wt. of fine gold was to be used.[62]

The rest of the Bill, however, was far more satisfactory to the Company. The proportions of gold and silver to be allowed to cover silk thread were as the Company had asked, and no copper, brass or other inferior metal was to be spun on silk. Best of all from the Trade's point of view no gold and silver thread lace fringe and other work as well as thread or work made of brass, copper or other inferior metal was to be imported into England, Wales or Berwick on Tweed (then still a border port between England and Scotland). The Company liked the Bill so much that it agreed to continue assisting it through the Lords.[63] It became law in 1698. It was originally passed for only three years but a similar act with an increase in penalties was passed on its expiry for a further seven years.[64] The Company also petitioned in the matter of the Buttonmakers bill. Button-making obviously represented an important outlying aspect of the trade,[65] that the Company should have given its support is an index of its vitality and interest in all aspects of the craft.

It is obvious from all this that the early officials of the Company, John Borrett the Clerk,[66] and Richard Brady[67] the Beadle, carried heavy responsibilities. John Borrett was a man of considerable standing. He was already the City Solicitor and obviously impressed the Company, which in the later minutes endowed him with the grandiloquent title of Protonothary.[68] He negotiated the Charter and the Byelaws and organised the Parliamentary lobbying which was so vital in the matter of the Gold and Silver wire-drawing Acts. After he had steered the Company through its early difficulties he handed over the appointment to his nephew, William Borrett, who acted first as his assistant in 1700/1 and then as full clerk in 1702.[69] The Company's relations with their first clerk remained friendly and the Court invited him to dinner in 1719.[70]

Richard Brady in a less exalted position acted as figure head for the early apprenticeships, was the summoner of all meetings, the enterer-up of apprenticeships, and general go-between. His annual salary was £10 which was regularised to a quarterly payment in 1694.[71]

There were many small administrative details to be dealt with in the early years. The Court at first seems to have been not quite clear about its own powers. In 1694 it sent Richard Brady to procure papers of instruction concerning apprentices from some other Company.[72] The members of the Court did not know who were the members of the Common Council and Richard Brady was asked to provide a list so they might study it.[73] Even more mundane things had to be done for the first time. A ledger for the accounts had to be bought in 1694.[74] Books for freedoms and minutes were not bought until 1698[75] although both sets of documents exist from 1693.[76]

Presumably they were made roughly and then fair-copied. The City seems to have been confused about the Company's status. In 1700/1 the City Chamberlain wrongly licensed John Osborne a foreigner,[77] i.e. not a freeman of the City but not necessarily an alien, as a Gold and Silver Wyre-Drawer, and as late as 1703 the Company had to send a caveat to the Chamberlain not to transfer Gold and Silver Wyre-Drawers without the consent of the Company.[78]

One difficulty to confront later clerks and beadles did not occur in these early years. The members of the Court may have been inexperienced but they were not dilatory or reluctant. The later reiterated resolutions that the hour glass shall stand on the table and that those who come after shall be fined and the everlasting adjournments of the Court for lack of a quorum were only adumbrated by minor complaints in 1701[79] that members were not attending Courts and that members were late.

The really great problem facing the Court and the officers alike was lack of funds. The City Companies founded earlier had attracted large benefactions in land, which with time and wise administration had greatly increased in value, and they were by this time very rich indeed. The Gold and Silver Wyre-Drawers had no such supplementary income and apart from the subscriptions made towards the Charter did not attract any further donations. This was partly because the medieval practice of leaving a proportion of an estate to charity had stopped by then. It was also because the Gold and Silver Wyre-Drawers, although men of substance, were without free capital. The trade, dealing as it did in luxury goods made of materials of high prime cost, needed a large capital investment in proportion to profit. It goes without saying that men with capital so invested would be chary of leaving legacies which their sons might only be able to pay to the detriment of their business.

The Company's income depended entirely on quarterages (i.e. the annual fee for membership payable quarterly by all freemen), fees from apprenticeships, freedoms and the holders of office, fines from offenders and from those refusing office. These were not neglible; the quarterage was 2s. per annum[80] and by 1715 there were 358 freemen.[81] Apprenticeship cost 2s. 6d., the freedom 3s. 4d., the office of Assistant £10. Fines for offenders ranged from £5 and 40s. for every month thereafter for those who practised the trade without being free[82] to 6s. 8d. for not binding apprentices.[83] The Company's income in 1700 was £79 12s. 6d.[84] This, however, was very little in comparison with its expenses which were £72 15s. 6d. The lobbying of Parliament and the administration and enforcement of the Byelaws cost considerable sums. Indeed, these were so heavy and the Company still so insecure in the exercise of its powers that a resolution was taken in 1698/9 that the actual searchers should be protected from prosecution; by the Company as a whole.[85]

An appeal was made for a subscription for the debts of the Company in 1701,[86] which solved the difficulty for a time. The debts were actually discharged by each member of the court making a contribution.[87] An attempt was made to help the Company's present difficulties by granting to members of the Court commutation of quarterage for life on payment of 20s.[88] Ten years purchase was a reasonably good bargain for the Company in view of the short life expectancy but it inevitably depleted future revenue.

Against this background it is impossible not to admire the courage and determination of the men who, so situated, prosecuted their cause with such application and administered their newly created powers so fearlessly. It is all the more remarkable in contrast to the Vintners' Company, which at this very period was finding it impossible to persuade members to volunteer to carry out the duties of search.[89] Of course, some of the reason was that the men at the head of the Company were executives in the trade itself and concerned with these matters because their livelihoods depended on them.

There were compensations; the trade was flourishing. Gold and silver wire was still very much in fashion and clothes increased both in elegance and in frequency of change of style. Competition from France, by this time a major rival, had decreased. The Revocation of the Edict of Nantes in October 1685 which deprived the Huguenots of their political power and separate organisation had harmed French manufacture, for many craftsmen of the Huguenot persuasion left the country taking their skills with them. That at least one of these was a Gold and Silver wire drawer is confirmed by the Company's own minutes. An alarmed report was made to the Court in 1703 that a Frenchman was working in London.[90] Unfortunately the minutes do not say whether this particular man later became free, although many later wire-drawers had names of French origin. The wars with France, King William's War 1689–97, and the War of the Spanish Succession 1703–1713, looked at first as if they might damage the trade. In the 1690s a Bill was introduced to forbid the wearing of gold and silver lace during the war with France. They did not do so. The Bill was not passed and the Wars by making French goods less accessible helped the home market.

IV

How the Company and the Trade flourished in the 18th Century

THE 18th CENTURY in Britain was a period of industrial revolution and social and political unrest. These developments were closely reflected in both the history of the trade and of the Company.

From 1716 there was a movement towards the use of machinery and the employment of craftsmen in factories, rather than outworkers. This was particularly the case in the textile trade which was technically more advanced for its period, and better capitalised than any other industry. The manufacture of silk yarn, for example, had been highly mechanised in Italy for many years, but the secret had been jealously guarded and the knowledge had not spread to Britain. In 1716 John Lombe on a trip to Italy managed to steal the plans and on his return to patent them.[1]

Similar movements were apparent in the gold and silver wire drawing industry. The industry which in the 17th century had been based on hand spinning, not even wheel spinning, by 1767 had become largely dominated by engine spinning. This produced some difficulties for the Company which was not sure at first whether such spinners might properly be accounted members of the Company. However, a vote of ten in favour over three against, resolved the question and the Company rigorously insisted on the enrolment of the work people concerned.[2] Nearly all of them were women,[3] although one man, Williams who was following the art of engine spinning in Cranbourne Alley, Leicester Fields, was sued because he had not followed the trade for seven years.[4] The employers of this female labour were, for the most part, men. Four men were summoned by the Court in 1767 for employing 'women who work at engine spinning',[5] but no woman is mentioned as an employer although one widow, Rebecca Smith, who was an engine spinner, took up her freedom in 1770 and may have been an employer as well as a craftsman.[6]

18th-century enlightenment and enterprise is shown, too, in the Company's willingness to accept foreigners with their greater skills. This was particularly true of Frenchmen. Among the names of those who were members of the Company, many are of French origin. Lewis Marquerier[7] and John Lewis Camroux[8] are only two of the most obvious examples, and as late as 1764 a Frenchman who produced a certificate saying he had served the King was considered for membership. In all fairness it must be admitted that he also offered to pay £10 for the privilege.[9]

The trade flourished more at this time than at any other, and until the change in fashion which followed the traumatic shock of the French Revolution in 1789, not only were clothes elaborate but also often changed style. Gold and silver lace were in great demand both for ceremonial dress and for day to day wear. The Windsor uniform designed by George III almost inevitably employed large quantities of gold lace,[10] but the Countess of Marr, on the evidence of her portrait painted in 1715, also trimmed her riding habit with elaborate and heavy silver lace.[11] Not, one would have imagined, very practical. Perhaps she was a decorative rider rather than a hard goer. Goods seized by the Company as being of inferior quality in 1766 at James Aytom's and John Bruce's tailors, by Francis Lycett and William Kew, are listed as a 'brocaded silver and gold coat, a pair of breeches, $2\frac{1}{2}$ dozen silver coat, $2\frac{1}{2}$ dozen silver breast buttons, and 10 gold breast buttons'.[12] Dresses for special occasions could cost as much as 500 guineas, and a waistcoat alone might cost upward of fifty.[13] Towards the end of the period the most absurd styles were adopted by the fashionable. The men of the species earned themselves the style and title of Maccaronis, in consideration of their affectation of foreign manners and customs. One of these exquisites appeared in the Assembly Rooms at Bath arrayed 'in a shot silk coat, pink satin waistcoat, breeches covered in a silver net, white stockings with pink clocks and pink satin shoes with large pearl buckles, his hair was dressed very high and stuck full of pearl pins'. Ridiculous or not, it was all good for trade.[14]

Naturally the importance of the trade was reflected in the affairs of the Company. The increase and growth of trade imposed greater duties of search and oversight. The Company's interference in this way was not always welcome and the cost of so much administration was always high. In 1747/8 the Company made a special resolution to indemnify the Master and Wardens and informers from the expense of siezing French lace and embroidery.[15] In 1768 Mr. Kennedy and Mr. Bevan were awarded £20 for their trouble and the other two officers for helping the Company to apprehend one Shütz. Kennedy and Bevan were probably Sherriffs' Officers and were certainly avaricious, since even so large a sum did not satisfy them. The Court Book relates that they went away very abruptly saying that when the Company wanted them they might send for them.[16] In 1761 Gratuities paid to those helping in the siezing of blown lace included five guineas to the coachman, two guineas to the Ostler and a guinea each to Mr. Dell and Mr. Smith.[17] Dell and Smith, unlike Kennedy and Bevan, were Members of the Company and were later employed by the Company in other ways.[18]

With the exercise of the Company's powers came the welcome recognition by the Government of the Company's expertise and usefulness. In 1764 the Commissioners of Customs asked that someone should go three times a week to inspect foreign lace. The Company agreed, and Mr Low was asked by the Company to attend and represent them in this matter.[19] In 1765 the number of times he was asked to attend was reduced to twice a week,[20] but the Company continued to accommodate the Commissioners of Customs. In 1766 Mr. Dell was appointed to attend instead of Mr. Low.[21] In 1768 Smith, a weaver, was given two guineas[22] for attending the Custom house and Dell in the same year was given a gratuity of five pounds for a similar service.[23] In 1755 the Renter Warden spent 4s. 3d. at the Kings Arms and the Customs house when he went there to examine some silk imported from China;[24] an interesting example of the spread of 18th-century trade. At the beginning of the century the silk was coming from Turkey.[25]

The Company continued to protect its privileges and the interests of the Trade by lobbying Parliament about the imports of foreign manufacture and the quality of the British wares. By this time (1755) France had fully overtaken Italy as the major foreign rival. Interestingly enough, as in the case of the Venetian work, there was a certain amount of agitation about the superiority of the French work. This was attributed by John Waller, a practising wire-drawer, to the fact that the French metals were of better quality. According to his own account he knew something about it. He was a wire-drawer of some ingenuity, having invented a refined steel for use in making flatting rollers, and had actually demonstrated his findings as to the quality of English gold and silver to the Royal Society. He had also used his refined steel for making razors which were sold to gentlemen in Europe as well as the King of England and various members of the nobility and gentry. The Revocation of the Edict of Nantes had caused craftsmen to emigrate to Holland as well as to Britain; there was a gold and silver lace making industry at this time in Amsterdam. One of Waller's contacts, a Monsieur Chatalan, told him that his father had laid out above £3,000 in mills for flatting, which he had imported for the most part from Leipzig in Saxony.[26]

In 1720 the Court won a technical victory with the Commissioners of Excise. There was some question as to whether the duty imposed on plate was chargeable on gold and silver wire and the Commissioners, to the delight of the Company, ruled that it was not.[27]

In 1741, the previous Gold and Silver Wire Acts having expired, the Company campaigned successfully for a new one. The Act received the King's consent in 1742. It was very like the previous Acts, but had some interesting differences. No time limit was given. This in itself was a great victory for the Company, and must have saved some expense, since it made it unnecessary for the Company to lobby Parliament every time the Act expired. The Act also laid down that before the gold was applied for the making of gold wire, the silver ingot should be weighed in the presence of an officer of Excise and that it should be again weighed after the gilding, to ensure that the required quantity of gold, i.e. 4 dwt 4 grains per 1lb. troy, had been applied. Excluded from the Act was the fake gold and silver wire made from copper which was used in the theatre.[28]

The Court's greatest exertions were demanded by the Bill brought into the House by Lord Strange, Mr. Gibbon, and Mr. Sydenham to prohibit the wearing of gold and silver lace, thread or wire in apparel.[29] The Bill was read for the first time on 24 January 1743/4 and the Company immediately mobilised its defences. It managed to raise a very strong lobby. The Weavers' Company conferred with them and joined the defence, contributing no less than £50 in subscriptions towards the cost of opposing the Bill.[30] The Gold and Silver Wyre-Drawers' Company presented a petition.[31] The dealers in gold and silver lace, weavers and fringe makers presented a petition. The Church Wardens and Overseers of the Poor for the Parishes of St. Luke and St. Giles Cripplegate presented a petition.[32] The Bailiff, Wardens and Assistants of the Weavers' Company,[33] the manufacturers of gold and silver wire in the City of Coventry and the Mayor and Bailiffs of the same city, all presented petitions.[34] The Bill was dropped.[35]

So much support demonstrates the extent and strength of the Trade. Indeed, in the St. Luke and St. Giles petition, the Churchwardens and Overseers claimed that over 6,000 persons were engaged in the trade.[36] Despite the ecclesiastical functions of these personages one must reluctantly conclude that they were exaggerating, but even so, one can assume that those in the trade must have been fairly numerous to galvanise the petition at all. The petition from Coventry is most interesting, since it shows a geographic spread and that there was a sufficient number of workers involved to encourage the Mayor and Bailiffs to join in the petition.

With so many financial calls on it the Company could not afford to neglect the enforcement of the payment of the quarterage dues. The original idea was that members should come quarterly to the Hall and pay their dues with voluntary goodwill. Unfortunately the members seem to have been forgetful of their obligations, and by 1720 the court had found it necessary to organise collections. The collections were made by the Master and one of the Wardens assisted by several members and the Beadle. The collectors were divided into two parties, presumably with the Master in one and the Warden in the other. One of the parties collected from the freemen living in Aldgate, Southwark, the Royal Exchange and Moorfields. The other party collected in Cripplegate. All the collectors were to meet at the Globe Tavern, near Stocks Market at 3 o'clock to dine.[37] It is interesting that Cripplegate formed a collecting area of its own, and suggests that the Churchwardens and Overseers of St. Giles's, and St. Luke's were right in declaring that many gold and silver wire-drawers were resident in their parishes. It also seems like a late survival of the medieval organisation of the City, when trades were concentrated in various streets and areas and gave the City many of its present day names, such as Milk Street, and Honey Pot Lane. The medieval Vintners, for example, were located in the Vintry, the Salters in the parish of All Saints Bread Street.

The Company may have been interested in its financial affairs, and how should it not have been, but it was not neglectful of its charitable and social duties. Members of the Court such as poor Mr. Glyde in 1761[38] had their fines returned when they fell on hard times. Apprentices were protected as well as reproved and, in 1729, an order was obtained from the Lord Mayor and Aldermen releasing one Samuel Turner from the service of Jeremiah Walton because of Jeremiah's use of 'immoderate' means to correct him.[39] In order to safeguard the apprentice as much as the Company's own fees, the Company was careful to make sure that all apprentices were properly indentured and enrolled. Not all Masters were as amiable as Joseph Brown who, when summoned for his failure to register his apprentice, disarmingly acknowledged that he had wrongfully bound an apprentice to the Grocers' Company but plaintively added that he feared no man would stand trial with the Company and protested that he never would not bind any apprentice to the Company again.[40] In 1766 George Rivers, with some spirit, was impudent in the matter of his apprentice;[41] and in the same year, William Clayton was even more explicit in his reply. He was summoned for employing Samuel Bradford, not being free of the Company, but he was quite unaffected by this and declared he would 'set Bradford to work the next day and would likewise bind a boy at Weavers' Hall'. Further, he did not care what the Company could do.[42] In fact, Rivers and Clayton both submitted in the end and the matter was composed. Not so simple was the affair of John Lewis Camroux. Camroux had been apprenticed to Richard Miflin, but when Miflin went to Ludgate for debt in 1769, he was left without a Master. Mrs. Miflin, who presumably wished to keep the services of Camroux against Miflin's return, complained to the Court that Charles Bull, the creditor who had had Miflin put in Ludgate, had also illegally engaged his apprentice and set him to work. Bull was at first reluctant to admit this, but after contradictory evidence supplied by a Mr. Hanmaker finally admitted that he had received the profit from Camroux's work for 13 weeks.[43] The Company resolved the matter from its own point of view by transferring Camroux from Miflin to Bull,[44] and so Mrs. Miflin had her revenge for the suing of her husband, but still lost the apprentice. In fact, the matter did not end there; when Camroux wished to take up his freedom in 1771 he was at first refused by the Court on the grounds that he had not served a regular apprenticeship. Mrs. Bull came forward and swore that Camroux had served her first husband, presumably one Thomas Collins who was given as his first master, after the manner of an apprentice and took no wages as she knew or believed: but Mr. Bull, despite his earlier admission, refused to take the oath or give evidence. The Court having by this time taken Bull's measure, since the Minute book remarks that he behaved very bad to the Company as usual and abused the Clerk very much for drawing up the oath,[45] wisely decided to set aside formality. Camroux was made free on 8 August 1771.[46]

The matter of apprentices was to become a difficult one. The Company had bound itself in the Byelaws to a limitation of the number of apprentices to two for every freeman at any one time. This had been done partly in response to the demands of the working wire drawers and partly in response to the Company's own views on the social desirability of restrictive practices. The Court carefully explained these views in the following terms: 'It was so that the youth put out to the said trade as apprentices might, after they had served a laborious apprenticeship, be able to live and support themselves and families as journeymen in a comfortable manner, as persons in such a situation of life might reasonably thinking expect or deserve, without encroaching or imposing upon the master, members of the said Company for exhorbitant wages.' A thing which obviously struck very near to the hearts of the Court at the time for then they added: 'the bane and destruction of all Arts and Mysteries'.[47] Unfortunately, the Journeymen had not understood the beneficent legislation in this way and indeed had taken advantage of it; by 1761 it became necessary to do something about it. The journeymen, in the words of the Court, had risen to such 'an intolerable, insufferable and height of self sufficiency as to lead to disobedience and misbehaviour towards the Masters' that they were demanding most unreasonable wages (one suspects this was the crux of the matter), but for good measure were also 'losing the time of their masters by frequent and almost continued rioting, drunkenness and debauchery'. They were also—and here was the really heinous crime—'engaging in combinations and confederacies' (in modern terms, a trade union).[48] Such a situation was not to be tolerated and the Company retaliated by trying to increase the labour market. The Byelaws were altered so that henceforth the Master, Wardens and Court of Assistants were to be allowed three apprentices instead of two.[49] Not, one would have thought, a very drastic measure to take, considering the enormity of the threat.

In fact the measure was not sufficient and in the end became unnecessary. The Byelaw passed in 1761 had to be rescinded in 1774 as the trade began to decline.[50] As far as controlling the journeymen was concerned it was valueless. The temper of the times had altered with increasing industrialisation and acceleration in the rate of social change. This was particularly so of the period between 1750 and 1770. Craftsmen and artisans, hitherto content to submit to the kindly paternalistic social administration of the medieval system, became literate and politically aware.[51] The illegal imprisonment and ejection of John Wilkes by a corrupt Parliament alarmed such men for the future of the Constitution, and London rose in fury.[52] It was natural that such men should also combine for their own advantage and should reject the old city systems of control. This new vitality in a class hitherto submissive was reflected in ways less honourable. The John Gordon Riots in 1780 were the most savage London riots of the 18th century, and for days London was at the mercy of the mob. They caused just fear and distaste among all moderate citizens (incidentally, not excluding John Wilkes),[53] a fear which has been vividly immortalised by Dickens in *Barnaby Rudge*.

The City and the Company realised that its only approach must be one of conciliation towards the journeymen. An attempt by one Pitcher in 1789 to break the journeymen's monopoly by gaining permission to licence foreigners[54] (that is, anyone not a member of the Company not necessarily an alien) through the Aldermen's Court was refused by the Aldermen and resisted by the Company. Incidentally, this use of other labour to break strikes became a favourite tactic of industrialists in the 19th century. Perhaps one need go no further than Mrs. Gaskell's vivid description in *North and South* of the hatred of the northern workers for the Irish imported labour which was brought in against them.[55] In the City, however, and with Pitcher these methods were disallowed. Indeed, the Court of Aldermen proposed a conciliation settlement with the journeymen which was to give them new rates of pay. The new wages were to be the following:

	Gold			*Silver*	
Bright	20d.	1s per oz	for	16d.	8 per oz
Rich	20d.	11½d.	Bright	14d.	7d.
Ordinary	20d.	11d.	Fine	14d.	7d.
Fine	18d.	10½d.	Common	14d.	5½d.
Common	18d.	9d.	Bright	12d.	5½d.
	16d.	7d.	Common	12d.	4½d.
	14d.	6d.		10d.	3½d.
	12d.	4d.		8d.	3d.
	10d.	3d.		6d.	2½d.
				4d.	2d.
Allowance for waste 1s.			Allowance for waste 3d.[56]		

The Company's difficulties with Pitcher, however, were not over. He was a man of some determination, and, having failed with the Court of Aldermen, continued to employ foreigners on his own initiative.⁵⁷ When the Company remonstrated with him, he wrote back in the following terms: 'Gentlemen I have received a summons from you which appears to charge me with infringing some law of which I have no knowledge and which calls upon me to pay a penalty the which supposing it to be incurred I conceive you have no authority to levy on me'.⁵⁸ The Court, which had already fortified itself by obtaining counsel's opinion⁵⁹ on the matter, paid no attention to such bombast and merely sent a copy of the relevant Byelaw.⁶⁰ Pitcher, however, then proceeded to another tactic. He petitioned to be made one of the Art Masters of Bridewell.⁶¹ Because Bridewell was a house of correction and a work house this would have meant that he could teach the trade to any number of people not properly apprenticed and this would have given him a cheap labour force on the back of what was then the equivalent of the Social Security System. It was really like the dispute which still exists between the Trades Unions and those social reformers who believe that proper employment should be given to people in gaol. The Company was again too powerful and their petition against him to the Master's of Bridewell was successful.⁶² Pitcher was not appointed and the Company for the time being had preserved its monopoly.

The 18th century saw the first benefactions for the Company. These were not large, but were welcome none the less: a legacy of £10 for a silver tankard, which the Company still owns, from Christopher Blower in 1716;⁶³ a legacy of £100 from Mathew Abell (Abott) in 1735;⁶⁴ £40 from John Court in 1758.⁶⁵ In 1724 a Mrs. Christian Russell left a legacy of £100 and a silver salver. The legacy was to be used to pay £5 every year on New Year's Day to five poor widows, but the silver salver was to be for the Company's own use.⁶⁶ Mrs. Russell was herself a widow and had exercised her privilege to take up the freedom on her husband's death;⁶⁷ doubtless this explains both her care and her gratitude. The Company still uses a salver known as the Mrs. Christian Russell Salver.

The Company continued to attend to its more formal duties and splendours. A Common Seal in silver representing the Company's Arms was presented by Nicholas Cunliffe in 1741,⁶⁸ and is still in the Company's possession.⁶⁹ Nicholas Cunliffe was at the time one of the Wardens and became Master in 1743.⁷⁰ An interesting sidelight on the matter is that the Company used these arms illegally and did not properly register them until 1975.⁷¹ This despite the fact that William Berry, Registrar's Clerk to the College of Arms, gives a description of the Arms in his *Encyclopaedia Heraldica* in 1828.⁷² It was the more strange for the Company to behave in such a cavalier way since it had had dealings with the College as early as 1719,⁷³ when the court delivered a copy of the title of the Charter of Incorporation to Mr. Peers Mauduitt of the Herald's Office in order to have it inserted in Stow's *Survey of London* which it was intended to reprint. Alas, the College or at any event Mr. Mauduitt, seems to have been as neglectful of the Company as the Company was of the College for although an appendix to Stow appeared in 1720 the information supplied by the Company was not included.⁷⁴

The Company suffered no other retaliation from the College, if indeed this could be accounted one, and continued to use and display its Arms with insouciance and frequency. In 1788 Mr. Burnett presented it with three woodcuts of its Arms which the Company were pleased to accept,[75] and Lord Mayor's days throughout the 19th century were given greater glory by the display of the Company's banner.

It is ironical that the Company, so careful of its own privileges and duties, should have been so disrespectful to the rights of the College. What is even more remarkable is that the Company was able to enforce its powers whereas the College because of the decay of the enforcing body, the Court of Chivalry, was unable to compel similar obedience.[76]

Not all the Company's preoccupations were serious or formal; the lighter side of life received its due measure. The Byelaws had provided for the appointment of three stewards who were to give two dinners a year at their own costs. One of the dinners was to be held on Lord Mayor's Day and one was to be held on the election of the Master and was to be called the Election Dinner.[77] These dinners were originally given only to the Court with occasional guests such as John Borrett, the first clerk, or the sureties for the Renter Wardens,[78] but when a Livery was granted then the Livery came to be invited also.[79] It had naturally occurred to the Court that there might be some reluctance from freemen chosen to be stewards to undertake so expensive an affair, so the Byelaws also fixed an unusually large fine of £15 for those refusing to serve.[80] Only one such so chosen had the ingenuity to escape by declaring he was not worth £20 and therefore went unpunished.[81] In fact the fine of £15 was more than adequate. As late as 1761 Joseph Brown refused to serve but compounded when it was explained that his share of the expenses was only £7 13s. 10d. He obviously preferred to pay this in preference to £15.[82]

If Joseph Brown's share amounted to £7 13s. 10d., then the full amount for the dinners must have been £21 11s. 6d., an average per dinner of around £10 15s. 0d. For this the Company did very well. The menu for 1731 gives a first course of 3 dishes of fowls with oysters and forced meat balls, 3 chines (i.e. ribs of beef), 3 dishes of tongues and udders, 3 turkeys and 3 hindquarters of lamb and spinach. The second course was 3 dishes of ducks and larks, 3 dishes of minced pies, 3 forequarters of lamb, 3 dishes of salad and three stands of fruit and oranges and lemons.[83] Wine was ad libitum. However by 1791, and after the admission of the Livery, the Company limited the consumption to one bottle per head.[84] The menus did not vary much. Turkeys were sometimes added and geese substituted for the hindquarters of lamb. Forequarters of lamb were replaced by marrow puddings and larks were sometimes omitted.[85] As time went on the menus seem to have become almost traditional, like that for Christmas Dinner today. In 1766 a decision of the stewards to substitute tansy puddings for marrow puddings had to be agreed formally by the Court.[86]

For 60 years these dinners were held at the Half Moon Tavern in Cheapside and seem to have been uneventful enough.[87] In 1802, however, the Court decided to move to the George and Vulture Tavern in Cheapside, and things livened up considerably.[88] In 1808 the Court received charges from the George and Vulture for glass, china and other articles broken by the exuberant diners at the dinner held on 14 January.[89] The Company had begun to take itself for granted.

The highlight of the Company's history as an established organisation came in 1780 when a Livery was granted. This was a long cherished wish of the Company, provided for in the Charter of Incorporation[90] and mooted many times, particularly in the 1720s.[91] For one reason or another, probably poverty and insecurity, the matter had been deferred, but by 1780 the Company could boast that divers of its members were of considerable substance and that the Company represented a valuable and extensive branch of the British trade.[92] Even so, the money for paying for the petition and grant had to be raised by subscription, but with the proviso that, if the attempt were successful, then the money raised should be counted as a part of the livery fine.[93] With the help of the clerks in the Town Clerk's office whom the Company rewarded with £10[94] the Livery was granted in November 1780 and the Company achieved an equal standing with other city companies and the right for its members to take a full part in the government of the City. Even today it is only liverymen who may vote for the Lord Mayor and the Sheriffs.

The Company also acquired a not unwelcome new source of revenue. The livery fine which had been provided for in the Charter was fixed at £15, with payments in addition of 5s. 0d. to the Clerk and 2s. 6d. to the Beadle. The number of liverymen was limited to a hundred.[95]

Even so, there were straws in the wind which demonstrated the beginnings of a shift of emphasis, which was to turn a vital trading body into a city institution more involved in politics than trade with a membership not of craftsmen but of influential city magnates more likely to buy and wear the products of the wire drawer's art than to make them. The trade had begun to decline already—so that the 1761 Byelaw, which had allowed an increase in apprentices, had to be rescinded in 1774[96]—and it was to be almost annihilated by the change in fashions which followed the organic shock of the French Revolution. In the petition against Pitcher to the Masters of Bridewell, the Court mentions the decline of the Trade as one of its reasons for opposing him and states that the wire drawers trade did not employ more than 50 members of the Company.[97] The petition itself shows the social shift that was hoped for and indeed attained. It states that if a Livery is granted then many merchants, warehousemen and other traders, exporters of gold and silver lace, although not makers thereof would become members of the said company, the same being on a respected footing equal with the rest of their fellow citizens who are entitled to the benefit of privileges which by the custom of the city can be enjoyed by the liverymen only,[98] notably the right to vote, as above.

In 1780, however, the possibility of the French Revolution was hardly thought of, the change in dress which was to follow it unimagined. The Gold and Silver Wyre-Drawers rejoiced in their new status and bought a staff with a silver head.[99]

V

How the Trade and the Company changed in the 19th Century

ON 14 JULY 1789 the French guards and the small workshop masters and journeymen from the Faubourg St. Antoine captured the Bastille, thereby immortalising themselves in popular legend as the deliverers of the poor and the inaugurators of the French Revolution.[1]

Whether or not this event really deserved the significance attached to it in the popular mind is of no importance to this history, since the effects of the Revolution itself on European and British thought were profound. They were not only profound they were also immediate; so immediate that they were reflected in a thing as everyday as dress. Fashions altered radically and the trade in gold and silver wire fell off. So eminent a man as Charles James Fox, who had been known as a dandy in his youth, affected an extreme negligence in dress in sympathy with the extreme democratic prejudices of the Revolution.[2] Less important mortals, while maintaining cleanliness and decorum, abandoned the more elaborate forms of decorations. Even the most particular relied on the tailor's rather than the embroiderer's art to demonstrate the elegance of their taste. Queen Charlotte on her marriage to George III in 1761 wore a silver tissue-stiffened bodied gown embroidered and trimmed with silver and a purple and velvet mantle laced with gold.[3] Queen Victoria on her marriage to Prince Albert in 1840 wore white satin, orange blossoms, and Honiton Lace.[4] In 1770 a mere gentleman, Jacob Houblon, wore white and silver while his bride was splendid in silver muslin with a silver blond hat and cap. The bridesmaid wore a dress of white lustring ornamented with silver blond.[5] In 1776 Lord Stormont was married in a brown coat lined with couleur de paille and embroidered with foils. His waiscoat, also in couleur de paille, was embroidered with gold and foils.[6] In 1812 the bride herself was content with lace over white satin, ostrich feathers and swansdown.[7] Bridegrooms with no military standing became ever more sombre as the 19th century progressed, declining from the relative splendour of conventional evening dress to the everyday drabness of a morning coat.[8]

In ordinary day to day wear the use of gold and silver wire survived only in certain limited areas. The military services, as they do to this day, continued to use gold and silver wire. When in 1840 the 11th Light Dragoons, under the command of the Earl of Cardigan who was later to distinguish himself at Balaclava, were promoted to the 11th. Hussars, Prince Albert's Own (The Cherry Pickers), much valuable work was given to the trade. The new uniforms were of unusual splendour, the jackets were edged with gold lace, the cuffs were braided and ornamented with the same, the sword belts were resplendent with gold and the very saddle cloths were decorated with silver lace.[9]

Other occupations continued to use gold and silver wire. Game keepers still sported their traditional dress of green coats and gold laced hats. Beadles and Postmen were bright with gold and silver throughout the 19th century.[10] Even today Heralds and Judges, Admirals and Lord Mayors, Chancellors of Universities and Commissionaires of cinemas, the Queen herself at her Coronation and when she opens Parliament, continue to delight the eye with the splendours of the wiredrawer's art.

Nevertheless the trade did contract. The dire predictions of the Company in 1790 (see Chapter IV) were more than fulfilled. At the same time the Company lost heart and interest in the trade, stopped exercising its duties of supervision and correction, and abandoned its highly successful parliamentary lobbying. The Bill introduced in 1787, to make more effectual the Act of George II, was passed unaided by the Company. Barrett and Corney, who were one of the most successful firms in the 18th and 19th centuries, paid their douceur direct to 'a member of the Committee for getting the Act of Parliament passed to prevent counterfeit lace'. It was a reasonably substantial sum, seven guineas.[11] For this apparent indolence there were three reasons: the increased status of the Company as a livery company which resulted in a new membership, grander indeed but less intimately connected with wire drawing itself; changing attitudes to city government; and changes in the trade itself.

The petition for the livery foreshadowed the first of these reasons when it explained that the intention of the Company in asking for a livery was thereby to attract to itself 'merchants, warehousemen and other traders exporters of gold and silver lace although not makers thereof'. Indeed, as the 19th century progressed fewer and fewer freemen were connected with the trade at all. One of the most famous, Michael Solomon, was a leghorn hat manufacturer[12] and others were Members of Parliament and Army officers.[13]

Changing attitudes to the city government made all city companies reluctant to use powers which, if not actually valueless, were difficult to prosecute in the courts. Not least was this so in a company such as the Gold and Silver Wyre Drawers where finance was a problem. Fashionable thought was tending more and more to recognise only Parliamentary authority, and this was reflected in the deliberations of the Court. In a little less than twenty years the Company, which in 1791 had vigorously pursued Pitcher's illegalities and had confidently taken counsel's opinion, was so low in interest and morale that in 1810 a Committee set up to enquire into the privilege nonchalantly replied that 'it did not understand it and had no answer to the Court's enquiry'.[14] The Court with equal carelessness did not pursue the matter further.

The changes in the trade particularly affected the Company in that they caused the movement of the trade to other centres. Some of the trade, as we have already seen, had moved to Coventry in the 18th century but in the 19th century the use of gold thread for cotton headings in what was known as the 'Lancashire Trade', but which also included Glasgow and Northern Ireland, caused the movement of a large part of the manufacture of gold thread to more convenient centres, most notably Preston in Lancashire.[15] Some of these industrialists later joined the Company, but rather from courtesy and benevolence than any other reason.[16] It was not to be expected that these independent, self made northern businessmen would take much practical notice of a southern based, and to them archaic, institution.

Sadly, the Company not only lost control of the trade, failed to care for its privilege, and stopped exercising its watching brief on the activities of Parliament, but also suffered a crisis of morale in other ways. Meeting after meeting was adjourned for lack of a quorum or for insufficiency of business.[17] Mr. Assistant William King Wiggington, who had resigned his place on the Court to become Beadle in 1796,[18] behaved so badly in 1804 that he was formally reproved by the Court.[19] Worse than this, when William Robins, who had been Clerk for 42 years, died in 1820, the accounts were found to be deficient to the tune of £111 2s. 11d.[20] An attempt to make Mr. Reynolds, the Renter Warden for that year of account, make good the deficit came to nothing, but he made a token acknowledgement of his technical responsibility by contributing £20 towards the loss.[21]

This sad dereliction of duty by the Clerk probably explains one of the minor mysteries of the Company's history. The present Assistant Clerk, Mr. Norman Harding C.C., has discovered that the salver known as the Mrs. Christian Russell salver is not date marked as it should be, 1724 but is dated 1822 which is strange. It was the custom of the Company to include in its accounts the value of its silver, including this particular salver, as part of its assets. Very probably part of the missing £111 2s. 11d. was the value of the salver, which had obviously been lost during William Robins' tenure of office. It says much for the Company that at a time of such low fortunes it should have had so much true feeling as to replace the salver in kind so that Mrs. Russell's bequest should be preserved in the form in which she had left it, and her name be remembered in the manner she had wished.

Not only money and morale were lost at this time; things of even greater importance were mislaid. The Charter and Byelaws disappeared, but were fortunately rediscovered in 1822 at the George and Vulture;[22] left there doubtless by William Robins after a dinner.

It is not as though the Company deserved to be so badly treated by its officers. The Court's behaviour throughout seems to have been courteous and kindly. James Dennis the Beadle, who resigned in 1796 because of ill health, kept his full salary of £6 until he died[23] as indeed did the refractory James King Wiggington when he too resigned in 1809.[24] This at a time, too, when the Company was in financial difficulty. In 1800 expenditure had to be reduced and the Lord Mayor's dinner was discontinued.[25] A Committee conferred about cash difficulties in 1810 but the only solution it could suggest was that the livery should be increased and that the Master and Wardens should contribute 10s. 6d. to the cost of each of their guests at luncheons and dinners.[26]

Better times lay ahead. In 1824 a new clerk, Samuel Lepard, was appointed and he began to set matters right.[27] Indeed he served the Court so well and the Company was so grateful that he was made free and given the livery in 1827[28] and elected to the Court of Assistants in 1838.[29] Having unearthed the Charter and Byelaws he set about making a complete extract, and by the beginning of 1826 was taking Counsel's opinion.[30] A committee was formed to inspect the Company's records.[31] One Cordingley was threatened with being sued if he did not take up his freedom.[32] A petition was sent to the House of Commons to ask for the repeal of excise duties on the manufactures of the Company.[33] Meetings were regularised and were made to be held quarterly at the clerk's house.[34] Proceedings were taken against a certain Sparrow for not paying his fine and for not taking up his livery.[35] Other freemen were fined for not doing the same.[36] In 1832, the year he was Master, Ferdinand Richard Camroux, the owner of a surname quoted before in this chronicle, presented the Company with 'a highly finished framed painting of the armorial bearings' which was intended to be hung in the Court Room.[37] The Company still has no hall and at that time had no right to display Arms but the thought was kindly.

This was all very well but left the Company with two unresolved difficulties. The chronic shortage of funds and the need for a new function. As a partial solution to both difficulties the Court took a remarkably farsighted and sensible decision. It made free by purchase on 7 January 1831 Michael Solomon of 3 Sandys Street, Bishopsgate Street, a leghorn hat manufacturer by trade[38] and a Jew by race and religion. He was the first of his people to become a liveryman of the City of London.[39] He became an Assistant in the same year as his entry into the Company[40] and was Master in 1843.[41] He was elected to the Court of Common Council in 1832,[42] the year of the Great Reform Act.

He was grateful to the Company for its acceptance, and on his election to the Court of Common Council wrote a letter to his friends recommending the Company.[43] In the years that followed the Gold and Silver Wyre-Drawers were pleased to have many of Mr. Solomon's friends joining their fraternity: in 1833 Lewis Lazarus of 1 White Street, Cutler Street, Samuel Isaacs of 16 White Street, Lewis Isaacs of 6 White Street, Asher Isaacs of 11 White Street,[44] in 1834 Marcus Abrahams of 15 Bishopsgate Street[45] to mention only the first. These new members were all admitted by redemption, that is purchase, and brought by their fines much needed replenishment of the Company's funds; but more than this they gave their capacities and vitality to the Company, and with characteristic enthusiasm and intelligence played a dominant part in the new ceremonial, and city political rôle the Company came to adopt.

This ceremonial and political rôle was to show itself first of all in a greater participation in city shows and government and later on in the century in the chanelling of the members' varied capacities into the organisation of displays for the late 19th century orgy of exhibitions of which the Great Exhibition of 1851 was only the first.

The Company's first Common Councillor in 1832 was followed by even greater glories. Two Lord Mayors, Sir Polydore de Keyser in 1887, and Sir Henry Aaron Isaacs in 1889 and nine Sheriffs between the years 1885 and 1891 were members of the Company. At one time 10 members of the Court of Aldermen were also members of the Gold and Silver Wyre-Drawers.[46]

Naturally this increase in social and political standing in the Company resulted in a far greater involvement in City ceremonial. On 25 January 1838 the Court minutes note for the first time that 'twenty members of the Court stood in their livery gowns within the railings of St. Paul's on the occasion of the Queen's visit to the City of the 9th November 1837'.[47] This was when the Queen visited the city to dine at Guildhall

1. THE WIRE-DRAWING PROCESS AS PRACTISED TODAY AT STEPHEN SIMPSON'S WORKS AT PRESTON

Left: The rod being introduced into the drawhole

Below left: The bar being drawn through the drawhole with the grapple engaged in a link of the chain

Below right: The rod being drawn along the 60-foot length of the draw bench

2. The Royal School of Needlework's sampler for the Queen's Coronation Robe

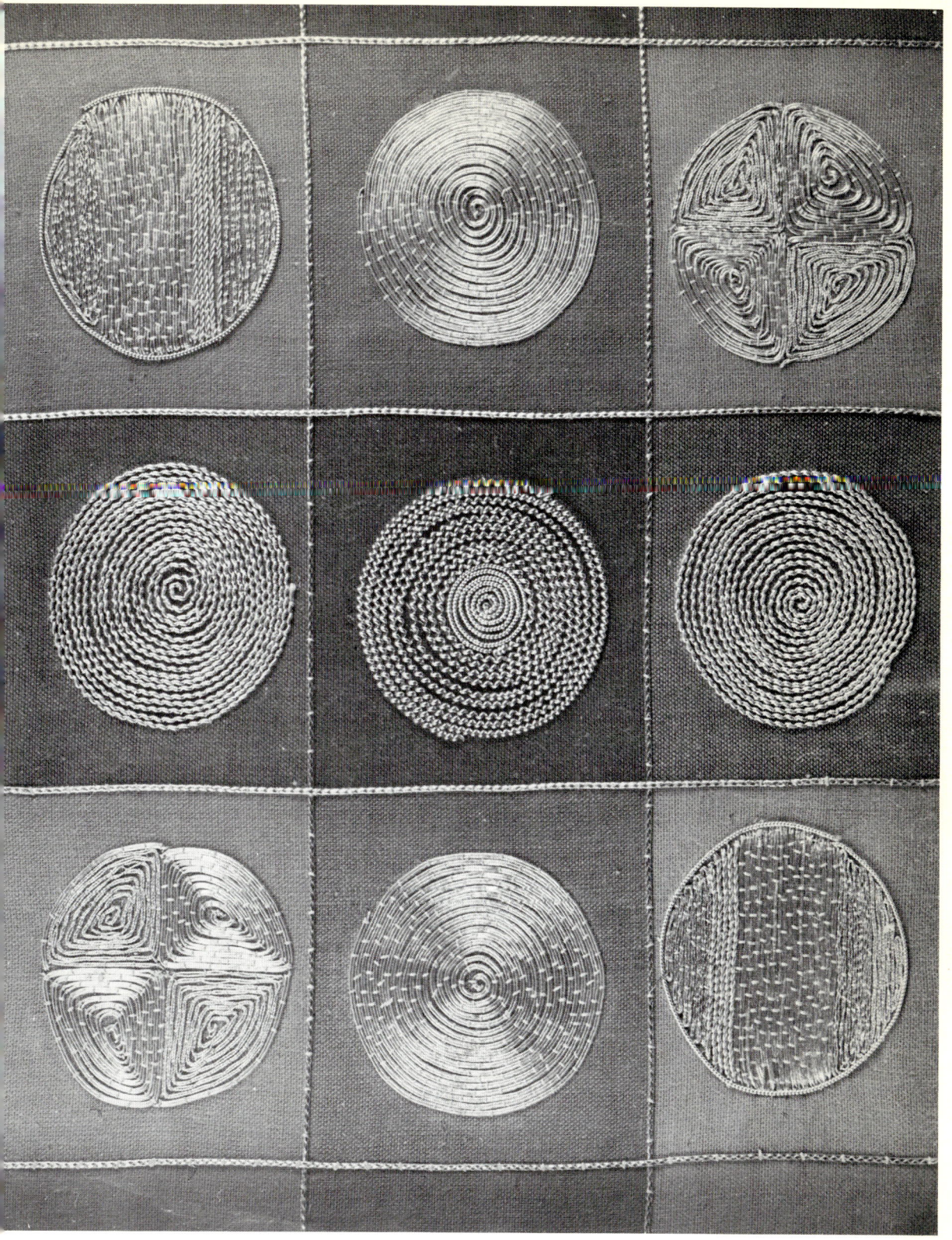
3. The Exemplar presented to the Company by Mr. Bernard Thorpe in 1967

4. *Above and below*: The first Charter of the Company dated 16 June 1693

5. Nicholas Southouse, Citizen and Gold and Silver Wyre-Drawer

6. The silver head of the Beadle's Mace which the Company bought in 1780. It is 17 inches high and weighs 32 oz.

7. Letterhead of Barrett & Corney

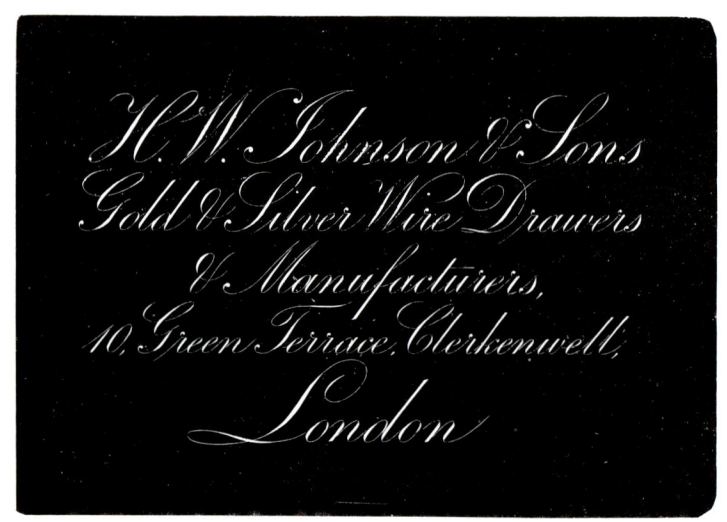

8. Letterhead of Benton & Johnson

9. The Company's Coat of Arms, granted in 1975

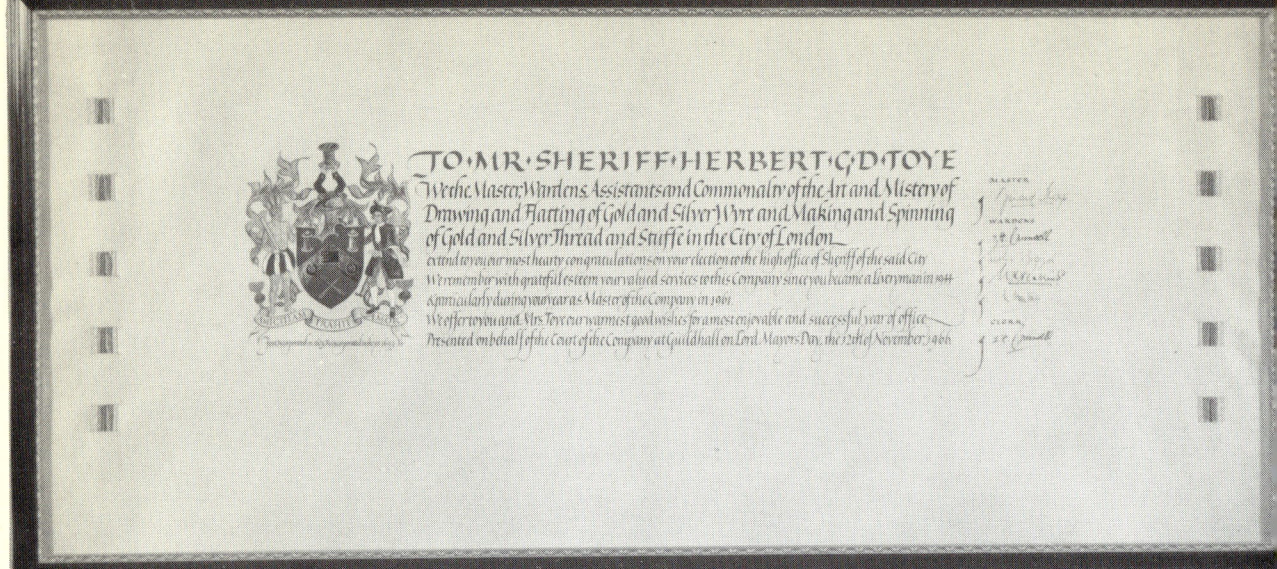

10. The illuminated address presented to Mr. Herbert Toye on his election as Sheriff of the City of London in 1966 (*Courtesy of Mr. Bryan Edward Toye*)

11. The badge presented by the Company to Mr. Sheriff Ralph Hedderwick in 1970

as the monarch customarily does after being crowned. A cold and chilly beginning, but one that was to be followed by great glories. In 1885 the Company took part in the Sheriffs' procession to Guildhall for the first time and later in the same year in the Lord Mayor's procession. 1885 was a truly wonderful year for the Company and celebrated with elaborate ceremonial. In particular the Company's trolleys in the pageant were eye-catching and effective. They showed how gold and silver wire drawing was practised at the time of the Company's incorporation, and were made and paid for by Mr. George Kenning, who was himself a practising member of the trade and a past master of the Company.[48] In 1887 the Company's first Lord Mayor, Sir Polydore de Keyser, was also accompanied with due ceremony.[49] The pomp included a Hungarian Band, rosettes to be worn and banners to be carried by those accompanying the procession and 21 chop dinners to sustain the participants afterwards.[50] The Company recognised the distinction Sir Polydore had given them by presenting him and Lady de Keyser with a silk screen embroidered with the Arms of the City in proper colours, and of course ornamented with gold and silver wire.[51] In 1888 the Company again took part in a Sheriff's procession from Clothworkers' Hall to Guildhall and in 1889 was again in the Lord Mayor's pageant. In 1889 the Gold and Silver Wyre-Drawers' contribution was given an historical and heraldic emphasis. The coachman and footmen were dressed in clothes resembling those of the Elizabethan period, ornamented with gold and silver lace, and the Master's carriage was accompanied by two men dressed to resemble the two unregistered supporters of the Company's Arms, an Indian and a Throwster.[52] The appearance of these two figures is familiar to modern liverymen and there can be no doubt that they would have lent an exotic and bizarre appearance to the Master's equipage. The sangfroid with which the Company used its Arms quite illegally casts a remarkable sidelight on 19th century attitudes to the past but the effect was doubtless magnificent. Magnificence was, as it should be, the order of the day and these 19th century Wyredrawers were men of their time, as little interested in the rights of the Court of Chivalry as they were in prosecuting their own privilege.

The practice given by the Lord Mayor's pageants served very well when the Company was asked to take part in the Great Victorian exhibitions. In particular the Company mounted successful displays at the International Health Exhibition in 1884[53] and at the Royal Military Exhibition in 1890.[54] The exhibits seem to have been of great interest and virtuosity. The display for the 1884 exhibition was placed in the part of the Hall called 'Old London Street'.[55] This street was a combination of the contributions of all the City Livery Companies and consisted of displays of the ancient crafts of each Company.[56] The Gold and Silver Wyre-Drawers' exhibit was given by, and made under the direction of, the same Mr. Kenning who had set up the Company's pageant for the Lord Mayor's Show.[57] The exhibit at the Royal Military Exhibition was a display of specimens of work in gold and silver wire and lace in their various stages of manufacture. In order to mount this exhibition the Company called not only on those members such as Mr. Kenning and Mr. Stewart, who were themselves connected with the trade, but also on members of the trade not in the Company.[58] This may seem a sad decline from the days of monopoly and dominance but does credit to the Company's good sense, and also incidentally shows how strong still were its trade affiliations. The names of the practising firms which are mentioned in this connection are of great interest and more is told of them in the next chapter. They were the firms of Kenning, Stanton, Benton and Johnson, Simpson and Rook, and J. B. Corney.[59] From these firms there were four representatives on the Court of Assistants: George Kenning, George Benton, Henry William Johnson, and Christopher Rook. Two Stantons, Edwin Alfred and Horace Frank, were liverymen,[60] and Stephen Simpson a member of the Preston family in partnership with Rook was to become a liveryman in 1920.[61] The Court was so delighted with the success of the Royal Military venture that it commissioned souvenir cards to be sent to all members of the Company and to those members of the trade who had helped with the exhibition. This card was designed by a Miss Ethel Wright.[62] The cost of the exhibition, which included the provision of a caretaker,[63] was so great when put with the other expenses of the year that the Company had to forgo the annual livery banquet but, if only for the good relations it cemented with the trade, it must have been worth it.[64]

Besides exhibiting its wares and itself in public the Company began to show some interest in its past. A sign in institutions as well as in people of comfortable establishment and middle age, but also in this instance typical of the period. It was fashionable at the end of the last century to be interested in histories and the Company duly commissioned its first. It was a very fashionable time. In choosing a member of their own Court, Horace Stewart, the other members could not have been more in keeping with the times, and it is doubtful if they could have been better served. Mr. Stewart was a true scholar in the best traditions of Victorian scholarship, erudite, a reader of documents not a romancer, painstaking and accurate. His work has been of great help in writing this history and it is impossible to imagine any subsequent history which would not rely heavily on his pioneering work. The history cost £95 5s. 0d. to print and was illustrated by Miss Estelle D'Avigdor, the daughter of one of the youngest liverymen. The Court were obviously delighted by her still charming drawings since they made her a small presentation. Alas, all we know about it, as the Court Book for this period is lost, is that it cost £2 17s. 0d. Mr. Stewart was presented with an illuminated address.[65]

Towards the end of the 19th century the Company was very jolly. If there was not a part to play in a Lord Mayor's procession or a Sheriff's, and there nearly always was, there was always the livery banquet. In 1891–2 there was even a ball. The livery banquets and dinners were held at the Albion tavern,[66] the Cannon Street Hotel[67] and the Criterion Restaurant.[68] The ball was at the Hotel Metropole and cost £427 6s. 0d. Double tickets cost £2 10s. 0d., gentlemen's tickets £1 5s. 0d. and ladies tickets only 15s. 0d. It is to be hoped that this prudent pricing resulted in the provision of a sufficient number of dancing partners for the gentlemen attending. The band of the 14th. Hussars supplied the music for the evening at a cost of £20 and a Swedish Sextet, the Zeruga Minstrels, Madame Pemberton Hinks and Miss Marie Douglas, among other distinguished artistes, entertained the guests.[69]

At this time what is now a long standing tradition was begun. In 1880 the Lord Mayor and Sheriffs attended the Company's banquet for the first time[70] and have done so every year ever since.

Of course all these parties were frivolous, but behind them lay a sound policy. It was not only right that the Company should celebrate its acceptance and safe establishment in the city hierarchy, it was also sensible. A company which has few funds and no benefactions to speak of depends on fines and fees for its revenue. If the Company is seen to be flourishing and politically important it will the more readily attract members, rich members and, more important even than this, potential benefactors. In this policy the Court was greatly encouraged by the Clerk, Wynne E. Baxter, Undersheriff of London, J.P., D.L. Mr. Stewart says he 'introduced many gentlemen of position and influence to the Company.'[71] The Court showed its appreciation of his services by having his portrait painted by Thomas Cave and presenting it to him. One member of the Court, Hymen Aaron Joseph C.C., Master three times from 1884–1886, introduced over fifty members to the Company.[72]

In this policy the Company had, however, one difficulty. The number of the livery had not been changed since it had been fixed in 1780 at one hundred. It was obvious, that if all these gentlemen of position and influence were to be welcomed as they should be, this number would have to be increased, and originally the Court asked the Court of Aldermen for an increase of 100% to two hundred. This the Aldermen were not prepared to do, but they did increase the number to one hundred and fifty. They also raised the admission fine from the 1780 figure of £15 to 25 guineas.[73]

Participation in the great Exhibitions of the period also had its value. The 19th century, like our own, was a period of over-legislation, parliamentary interference and popular attack on established bodies, particularly on rich established bodies since they seemed to offer heaven-sent opportunities for plunder and confiscation. In the City this popular agitation took the form of an attack on the funds and powers of the City Livery Companies. In consequence of the agitation two City Livery Companies' Commissions were appointed, one in 1834, and a more powerful one in 1881, to set the public mind at rest. In fact these enquiries failed to discover, even in the larger city companies, any sign of the expected corruption; indeed, most city companies in fact contributed far more to good works than they were obliged. The replies of the smaller ones were even more disappointing to the reformers.[74] In 1834 the clerk of the Gold and Silver Wyre-Drawers informed the Commissioners that the Company owned no real estate and had no funds, except those applied to charities, which were not derived from the fines and fees of its members. As we have seen, these were hardly sufficient for day to day running. The clerk's annual salary was £10 10s. 0d., the Beadle's £6.[75] In 1881 the replies were little different, although with the increase in membership the financial position had begun to improve.[76] The clerk's salary had been raised to £30 by 1893.[77] After many earnest deliberations and the publication of a monumental report, the 1881 Commission came to some conclusions and made two recommendations. These recommendations were put into effect by the Company. They were as follows; that charity accounts should be accounted separately in City Livery Company books, and that City Companies should interest themselves more fully in technical and trades education.[78] The Company had so few charitable funds that the first recommendation was hardly a difficulty, and the second was acted upon with speed and enthusiasm. We have already seen the success achieved by propaganda and advertisement, but even more generously the Company in 1890 set aside £105, 5s. 0d., eight per cent of its total capital, for the apprenticing of boys and girls in the trade of gold and silver wire drawing or in any connection therewith.[79]

At the end of the century the Company's affairs were in far better order than they had been at the beginning. Morale was high. The Company's prestige greatly enhanced. The investment capital stood at over double the £700 it had been in 1800. In 1882 the first investment in real estate was made by the purchase of freehold ground rents at 2 Barnsbury Square Islington for £410[80] and this was followed by the purchase of ground rents in Mortlake for £405 in 1898. This property brought in £16 per annum on 1–8 Agate Terrace, Worple Way South, 2 Queens Road and on 1 and 2 Rose Cottages, Rock Avenue.[81] The other investment capital stood at £1300 in the 1890's.

The Company's worldly goods had also increased. The greater wealth and status of the freemen had resulted in generous donations and benefactions in plate and objets d'art: the Camroux snuffbox, the Lindo ivory gavel, the Hepburn Rose Water dish, the Scovell Cup, to mention only a few.[82] The Company had celebrated its sense of corporate splendour by buying a gold and enamel badge for the Master in 1880[83] and its sense of corporate responsibility by buying a Poor Box in 1889.[84] The money for the Poor Box came out of corporate funds but the money for the badge was raised by a subscription of two guineas from each member of the Court. The badge was later fittingly augmented in 1891 by the presentation of a gold and enamel chain by Gabriel Lindo, Master of the Company for three years from 1889–1891.[85]

One cannot help but regret the bustling days of the 18th century. It is sad to see the decline from active industry and commerce to politics and ceremonial. Just the same, the Company in the 19th century had achieved a great deal, not least in bringing about this transition in such a quiet and very English way. The Assistants, Masters and Clerks of the 19th century, too, were worthy of their capable predecessors. They carried out the spirit of the Company's Charter even if they had to abandon the exercise of its powers. Friendly relations with the trade were sustained. Brotherly kindness within the fraternity was maintained. The dignity of the Company was increased. In 1755 the Renter Warden was busily engaged in inspecting silk imported from China.[86] In 1888 he was giving money towards famine relief in the same country.[87] I cannot imagine that either official would have quarrelled with the action of the other.

VI

How the Trade changed in the 19th and 20th Centuries and how it is organised today

OTHER REVOLUTIONS than the French were to affect the gold and silver wire-drawing industry in the 19th century. The Industrial Revolution changed its organisation, location and methods. New markets and uses were found. Towards the end of the century, as trade expanded within the British Empire, the products of the gold and silver wire-drawers' craft found world-wide outlets.

At the beginning of the century the trade was still centred on London. The archives of the only now existing gold and silver wire-drawing firm, Stephen Simpson (Est. 1829) Ltd., of Preston in Lancashire give the names of the following wire drawers still practising in London in the 1830s: Mr. Davies of Wood Street,[1] James Davies of 4 Gloucester Street, Clerkenwell,[2] John Thomas Javan, 14 Market Street, Clerkenwell,[3] Mr. Scovell of 28 Clerkenwell Close,[4] Messrs. Van of 9 and 10 Little Britain[5] and Henry William Johnson of Green Terrace, Clerkenwell.[6] At the end of the century the Company's own archives give the names of the following firms still actively engaged in the trade in London: Kenning's, Stanton's, Benton and Johnson, Simpson and Rook, and J. B. Corney.[7] The Johnson of Benton and Johnson was the grandson of Henry William.[8]

The archives of Stephen Simpson also mention a firm called Borrett and Borney as the major London manufacturers.[9] It seems likely, however, that Isaac Simpson's correspondent George Barton may have been mistaken and actually meant the firm of Barret and Cornie/Corney, a firm later to be represented by J. B. Corney. It is true that Barret and Corney were in a very nice way of business indeed and might well be mentioned by Mr. Garrard, the King's silversmith, as a firm to be trusted. The cash book of this Company dated 1785–1802 has lately been given to Dennis Johnson of Benton and Johnson by Mr. Roland Benton, the Gold and Silver Wyre-Drawers' oldest liveryman, and a descendant of the founder of Benton and Johnson.

The Cash Book is a fund of amusing and valuable information. The turnover of the firm for 1789 was enormous for that time; £3,396 18s. 5d. with an expenditure of only £148 13. 6½d.[10] Unfortunately the original partnership between Bryan Barret, his two sons John and Bryan Barret, and Thomas Corney was wound up in 1790 and a new partnership was formed between John Barret and Thomas Corney.[11] Thus it is that the book ends at a crucial point for estimating the effect of the French Revolution and the change of dress on the business of the firm. From the accounts, however, it seems unlikely that it would have been too disastrous for this particular business. By far the larger bills are for liveries and for military dress both of which were unaffected by the new fashions. The King's (George III's) bills for livery in 1789 were £649 18s. 7d. and £101 2s. 6½d. with a further charge of £143 16s. 7d. to the Master of the Horse (the Duke of Montagu). The King's bill for his own personal dress was only £69 1s. 6d.[12] In 1790 the Duke of Richmond's bills for stable livery were £1 17s. 0d. and 2s. 11d., for house livery 10s. 4d., and for his own dress 11d.[13] He was obviously not an extravagant man. The Marquess of Stafford's bill for liveries was £55 11s. 0d.[14] The Duke of Richmond in 1789 paid £10 4s. 0d. for liveries and only £3 17s. 4d. for personal dress.[15] The King's bill for the private hunt was £18 4s. 0d.[16] General Conway paid £389 17s. 1d. for uniforms for the regiment in 1787[17] and a further £387 4s. 11d. in the same year.[18] In 1790 he spent a further £194 3s. 7d.[19] General Boyd's officers spent £34 19s. 0d. in the same year.[20]

Of course, the rather charming small purchases would have disappeared with the fashions. The child's gold hat band which was the height of fashion in 1786[21] would not have been purchased five years later. On the other hand it is interesting to see the first adumbration of what was to become a most profitable side of the trade. In 1787 Barrett and Corney made and sold for 3s. 0d. the Friendly Order of St. Patrick on a green ribbon.[22] It was the forerunner of the quantities of Masonic Regalia made and sold today.

The firm had an extremely distinguished clientèle: the King (George III),[23] the Queen (Queen Charlotte),[24] the Prince of Wales (George IV),[25] the Duke of York[26] (who had ten thousand men), Prince Edward (the Duke of Kent),[27] Prince Charles of Mecklenburg,[28] Prince Ernest Augustus (the Duke of Cumberland, ill famed in Scotland as the 'Butcher'), Prince Augustus Frederick, Prince Adolphus Frederick,[29] the Duke of Devonshire,[30] Earl Cowper,[31] Lord Hardwick,[32] Lord Ashburnham,[33] the Duke of Richmond,[34] Lord Vernon,[35] Lord Trentham,[36] Lady Lennox[37] and the Duke of Montrose.[38] Jeremiah Bentham spent half a crown[39] and Mrs. Mytton, Squire Mytton's mother, had parcels sent by the Shrewsbury coach.[40] The Hon. George Petre, the six times great-grandson[41] of Sir John Petre mentioned in the second chapter of this book, also patronised the partnership.[42]

Barret and Corney seem to have been grateful for this patronage, perhaps unduly so, for the sons of George III were notorious for their inability to meet their debts. When the partnership was wound up, the Prince of Wales was still paying interest to the tune of £58 8s. 9d. on the bonds for his debts to the firm,[43] and the Duke of York was paying a bill of £800 by instalments.[44] However, the form which the gratitude took cannot have been other than delightful to the workpeople. On the occasions of the King's birthday,[45] the Prince of Wales' birthday,[46] the Duke of York's birthday,[47] the Duke of Gloucester's birthday[48] and the Duke of Devonshire's birthday[49] it was the pleasant custom of the partnership to adjourn to the Thatched House public house and to spend half a guinea on the refreshment provided there.[50] Beer was 3½d. a quart,[51] so the half a guinea was very adequate provision. When the King temporarily recovered his sanity in 1789 Barrett and Corney made an additional expedition to the Thatched House to spend a canonical half guinea.[52]

The clientèle was not only distinguished it was also wide spread. Parcels were sent by the Salisbury,[53] York,[54] Canterbury,[55] Liverpool,[56] Lincoln,[57] Brighton,[58] Rockingham,[59] Shrewsbury,[60] Doncaster,[61] Stamford,[62] and Arundel[63] coaches, as well as being delivered direct or collected by people's servants in London.[64] There seem to have been some foreign contacts also. The Cash Book records a payment of 1s. 6d. for a letter to Oporto in 1786[65] and of 1s. 0d. to the Foreign Postman in 1787.[66]

The firm dealt in all the usual gold and silver wire products. It made Windsor Hunt Lace,[67] tassells,[68] narrow gold and silver lace,[69] George lace,[70] gold fringe,[71] silver regimental Cartizanni lace,[72] gold tambour lace,[73] silver vellum lace,[74] gold flatworm,[75] silver marini lace,[76] broad silver scallop edge lace,[77] silver musgrave binding,[78] gold buttonhole thread,[79] sword knots,[80] silver bow fringe,[81] gold french orris lace,[82] black and silver lace,[83] gold twist,[84] spangles,[85] purls[86] and gold Prussian binding.[87]

The business employed a very small number of in-workers, all of whom were very highly paid. During the period covered by the surviving Receipt Book, 1785–1795, the firm employed Jacob Tibson at £60 per annum, Thomas Harrison at £57 per annum, J. Pendleton at £45 per annum[88] and Thomas Holmes at £12 a year.[89] They were all paid quarterly. The outworkers were paid on piece rates but also quite highly. Strangely enough only three of these outworkers were women,[90] but two of them have names of French origin: François Dujardin[91] and Ann Chaponier.[92] In 1785 Ann Chaponier was paid 12s. 5½d. for 30½ yards of gold and silver net.[93] One outworker, James Richards, was paid sums of £4 4s. 0d. and £10 10s. 0d. within three months[94] and others were paid sums as large as £41[95] and £34 15s. 0d.[96]

Other firms, too, even as late as the 1830s, were making a reasonable return on their capital. Van's, who were later bought out by a partnership consisting of Henry William Johnson and Isaac Simpson, were showing profits between £550 and £750 per annum in 1842.[97] Johnson, who was a fine wire drawer, (i.e. he bought the heavy wire drawn from bullion by Van's and converted it from $1/8$ in. thickness to the fineness of a hair) was showing profits of around £500.[98] Van's were selling upwards of 450 oz. per month in the West End as well as supplying Manchester and the Irish Trade.[99] The prices for gilt thread in London were 3s. 8d. to 3s. 10d. per oz. and 1s. 0d. at least per oz. profit could be made from copper plate. Henry William Johnson reckoned that the braid and gold and silver skeins also realised a pretty fair return at hardly any risk.[100]

The trade in London was of course stable and long established. Van's, who had traded first as Van Oort and Company and afterwards as Van and Turner, had been established for over a hundred years in 1842.[101] Henry William Johnson's firm was also of long standing.[102] When Roland Benton joined Benton and Johnson in 1901 the letter heading carried the proud boast 'established over a hundred years'.[103]

The partners in the London firms were active members of the Company. Joseph Johnson was master in 1821, Henry William in 1840, James Scovell was master in 1832, George Scovell in 1839.[104] The Turner family, with whom the Johnsons had been associated and who may have been the Turners of Van and Turner,[105] had many members who were masters. William Turner the elder in 1779, William Turner the younger in 1801 and Joseph Turner in 1804. Roland Benton's grandfather, George Benton, was Master in 1860.[106] Christopher Rook of Simpson and Rook was a member of the Court of Assistants in the 1890s.[107] Charles F. Corney was Master in

1863, Frederick Stanton in 1870 and George Kenning in 1882 and 1883. Luckily for the Company, many of the members of these old families have continued to take up their freedoms and liveries and to serve as masters. Roland Benton was Master in 1942 and Leslie W. Johnson in 1949. L. Murray, Dennis H. L., and Andrew Johnson, Leslie's three sons and the great, great grandsons of Henry William have all been Masters of the Company. Murray in 1958, Dennis in 1964 and Andrew in 1971. Members, too, have come from related trades. The Toye family of the firm of Toye, Kenning and Spencer Ltd., famous makers of masonic regalia, has had several members free of the Company. Herbert G. D. Toye was Master in 1961, and Herbert's brother, Frederick was a liveryman[108] B. E. Toye the Chairman of Toye, Kenning and Spencer, is a member of the Court of Assistants. The Toye family are perhaps the last family of Huguenot descent to be connected with the Company and the trade. Two members of the Firmin family of the firm of Firmin's, which has been famous for its manufacture of buttons since the reign of Queen Anne are liverymen of the Company. They are G. V. and J. W. Firmin.[109]

Throughout the 19th and well into the 20th century the London manufacturers kept the trade for laces and embroidery. This was so much so that when the Preston firm of Stephen Simpson ceased trading in partnership with the Johnsons, Stephen Simpson kept the London premises in Little Britain for this trade, and when the firm started its own embroidery department the skills had to be taught by the London House. Miss Beatrice Simpson and Miss Helen Simpson went to the London house of Stephen Simpson which had by then moved from Little Britain to the more fashionable address of 8 Warwick Street, Regent Street W.1, to learn the craft from the London manager, Lile Arthur Langmead, and the forewoman, Miss Hutchins.[110]

A daily cash sales book for Benton and Johnson 1884–1890 shows sales of gold tinsel, gold purls, gilt purls, smooth purls, rough purls, smooth passing, flatworm, silver purls, gold flatworm, gold pearl purl, plate, silver super lizandine pearl purl, gold bit spangles, silver slack twist, gold grecians, gold bright bullion, silver passing, silver number six passing, silver large breast spangles, wire check purl, sword knot lace, silver number seven Navy passing, gold wheat spangles, and gold grape spangles. The business was prosperous and Benton and Johnson were supplying large quantities of embroidery materials to a number of firms, among them Bailey's, Toye's, Simmond's, Barry's and the School of Embroidery in Lloyd Square.[111]

The skills of the craft were centred in London and Coventry until late in the century and even in some cases right into the twentieth. When Stephen Simpson began to draw wire in Preston in 1861 he imported Joseph Jefferies from London to start the large wire department.[112] In the fine wire department the fine wire was first drawn by a Londoner, William Ely Potter, who stayed with the firm and brought in his two sons to help him.[113] Other Londoners who helped in the early days in the fine wire department were Frederick William Smith and Thomas John Baverstock.[114] The firm of G. H. L. Tootell, established at the Springfield Works, Leyland, Preson in 1862, brought a man called Etherington from London to teach wire drawing.[115] The firm of John Sharp, also in Preston established in 1850 and bought by John Sharp in the 1870s, used a man called Charles Strike from London to install the first wire-drawing machinery. Charles Strike was a mechanic and designer of great natural ability. One secret of the craft, the making of pearl purl by machinery, was still only known by one firm, and that the London firm of Stanton's in Lewisham, until the 1920s. The secret was later acquired by John Sharp because of an interesting encounter. An ex-employee of Stanton's came to Preston trying to sell advertising space in the Sunday Pictorial. While touting for business he went to John Sharp's and in the course of the interview confided the secret to John Sharp's manager. From then on John Sharp's was the only firm of gold and silver wire-drawers which could make this particular kind of embroidery wire by machine. When Sharp's were bought by Stephen Simpson's in 1961 the secret passed to that firm.[116]

Lace making skills were centred in Coventry until the 1860s and Coventry continued to be the centre for the making of gold and silver lace until the 1920s. The firm of David Kenning's, which was taken over by Toye's, was one of the best known.[117] When Stephen Simpson began weaving gold lace by power in Preston in 1875 he went to inspect the Coventry ribbon machines and when he bought one of them he imported a Coventry man, William Rider, to install it.[118]

Despite its long tradition of dominance, its inherited skills and its obvious viability, the London trade was not as vigorous as it had been and in the 19th century it let pass the opportunity of a completely new market. It lost the chance to exploit what was called the 'Lancashire trade'. This trade was the sale of gold thread and plate for weaving into headings by the cotton industry, chiefly Jaconet mulls, sacarilla mulls and shirtings. These headings were woven into the end of a cut of cloth by varying lengths of picks, and formed an outline such as a pyramid. They were the distinguishing marks of the buyers in The India and China trade. Gold wire was used because it withstood bleaching. The heading was put in the cloth by the weaver and remained bright and plain after the cotton was bleached.[119] Stephen Simpson's reels carried a notice 'warranted to stand bleaching'.[120]

It was the proud boast of all the firms engaged in the 'Lancashire Trade' that no claim against the quality of the goods was ever paid. This was the more remarkable in that the weavers were required to pay the 2d. or 3d. each for the bobbins of gold thread themselves. The money was reimbursed but there must have been a temptation to substitute an inferior thread. Moreover the headings were very unpopular with the weavers because the loom had to be stopped to put them in and the weavers, who were paid on piece rates, lost the time.[121]

The length of thread or plate on a bobbin was either 52, 50, or 25 yards and was sold by what was called the pound. A pound was 104 bobbins but was packed in two pounds of 208 bobbins in the case of thread. Plate was made up in one pound packets of 192 bobbins. The finest wire used was 2,600 yards per oz. troy. The cotton used for the thread was polished 70/2 best Egyptian and dyed with a vegetable dye which disappeared in the bleaching process. The bobbins were coloured red, blue, green, or were left white and the ends were stamped with certain initials at the request of different customers.[122]

The Preston firms also made tambouring thread which was supplied to the bleachers. This was an imitation gold thread not guaranteed to withstand bleaching and was put into the cloth after this process. The design of the tambour was usually an emblem such as a leaf. The thread was sold by 1300, 1000, and 100 yards.[123]

The market for wire and thread for cotton headings in fact extended beyond Lancashire itself to Glasgow and Northern Ireland. It was used all over Lancashire. John Sharp's sold to mills in Blackburn, Darwen, Accrington and Great Harwood as well as in Preston itself.[124] Sharp's and Simpson's both had agents in Glasgow for their sales to the weaving trade and as early as 1833 Isaac Simpson's agent Mary Sutton, later Melling, later Taylor, mentions that there is an export market from Glasgow in gold thread to Belfast.[125] The cloth for which the headings were sold was intended for the India and China markets.[126]

Of course, the Lancashire firms who exploited the market for gold wire for use in cotton headings had the great advantage of geographic proximity and an intimate knowledge of the market. They did not, however, have the knowledge of the skills of the trade or the solid establishment of the London firms. With the coming of the railways and the establishment of a cheap postal service with rapid communication and easy carriage, particularly in a trade which was small in bulk, at least part of the loss of this market must be attributed to lack of initiative. When George Barton was looking for wire suitable for Isaac Simpson, the founder of Stephen Simpson, to flat in 1830, he was given the name of only one man, Mr. Scovell, who was likely to be able to fulfil his requirements.[127] In fact, George Barton did eventually find another, Henry William Johnson, who became Isaac's supplier and who spent many years in partnership with him.[128] Just the same the London manufacturers do not seem to have been very interested or eager. Henry William himself, delighted as he was at the prospect of purchasing Van's and a potential partnership with Isaac, still says in the same letter 'I don't care if I never do better'.[129] Isaac's sales representative in Glasgow, his sister Mary Sutton, wrote on 1 May 1833: 'There is a person in London that has sold to many in Glasgow that deals very largely in gold. Their orders would not be less than £100 worth at once and that very often and there is many of them has purchased from him'. This gentleman engaged in so apparently profitable a line had now given up business.[130]

Some of the London firms were lacking in real business interest and were unwilling to adopt new manufacturing methods. Barrett and Corney's business declined and when the last Barrett died the firm was bought out by Benton and Johnson. This was probably in the 1880s.[131] When Roland Benton joined Benton and Johnson in 1901 three of Corney's ex-employees were still on the staff. Powered machinery seems to have been a late development in the London trade. In Roland Benton's father's day the wire drawing machines were still man powered and if there was extra heavy work in drawing large silver bars, men were commandeered from the local gaol (Cold Bath Square Prison) to help turn the winch. The site of this gaol is now the Mount Pleasant Post Office. As late as 1901 the spangles were still being beaten out by hand. Mr. Benton describes the beater as 'a little old ladybird about four feet high'.[132]

The London trade was fixed in its ancient traditions and unwilling to change them. The factory methods were alien to it and enterprises with new machinery were foreign. For this reason the Lancashire manufacturers tended to look to London for skills but to Germany for machinery. Isaac Simpson's first rollers for flattening gold wire were bought from the German firm of Krupp.[133] Mr. Fitch, late of John Sharp's, remembers a pair of steel rollers from the same firm marked 'Krupp 1851' which were still in use when the firm was sold to Stephen Simpson.[134] Tootell's also bought from Germany from the firm of Konrad Danner.[135] The London Firms were also buying from Germany. There is still a pair of rollers at Benton and Johnson marked 'Krupp 1850'.

For the Lancashire firms, however, this was only a beginning. The owners were soon adapting and inventing new machines of their own and having them made in Lancashire. Isaac Simpson patented a machine for the manufacture of gold thread in 1853 which he had made in quantity for him by his nephew, Stephen Simpson of Mansfield.[136] Stephen, Isaac's son, invented a machine in 1869 for improving the methods of drawing fine wire.[137] The machine mentioned earlier which was imported from Coventry was copied and improved by him.[138] He designed and cut the pattern cards for the Jacquard looms which were used for making lace himself.[139] With the help of one of his early managers, William Chadderton, he constructed a machine for making purl from an old silk machine looking like a spinning wheel.[140] Stephen's elder son Isaac created a continuous drawing machine which completely revolutionised the process of gold and silver wire-drawing. Up to that time a separate machine had been necessary for each new size of wire. Isaac's machine could draw wire through numerous holes at the same time.[141]

The northern manufacturers, situated as they were among the great factory complexes of Lancashire, adopted factory methods and powered machinery from the first. It is true that Isaac Simpson started life as a clockmaker and when he began to flat wire did so on his own. His first employee, Martha Riley, was not engaged until 1836 and then she had to sign a solemn promise not to divulge the secrets of the trade.[142] However, by 1863 the number of those employed had risen to 41, all working in the factory at 42 Avenham Road. There were four men in the bar shed, a man and a girl in the silk room, 22 fine wire drawers and 13 spinners and flatters.[143] The drawing mill powered by a donkey had been replaced by steam by 1874.[144] The firm of G. H. L. Tootell, established in 1862, used steam power from the first.[145]

The factories of the northern firms were built according to a common pattern, and the works of Stephen Simpson still standing in Avenham Road are of great architectural interest. There is a substantial residence facing the road in which the founder of the firm lived until 1854, the better to attend to his business and watch his workmen,[146] and a courtyard at the back surrounded by factory buildings. It is exactly like the works of Mr. Thurston described by Mrs. Gaskell in *North and South* and typical of many such buildings.[147]

It is fashionable to deplore the effects of the Industrial Revolution on the quality of life of the working class. Even if this were so, it would be pure utopianism to argue that the London manufacturers were more noble in resisting industrialisation than their energetic and self-seeking northern counterparts. In fact it is not so. The cottage industries had been and in the 19th century still were greater exploiters, particularly of women and children than the factory industries ever were. It is true that one of Simpson's earliest employees, Isabella Ellen Boast, came to work at the tender age of 11 in 1865,[148] but in the 1860's the Devonshire, Buckinghamshire, Bedfordshire and Northamptonshire lace-making industries were employing children of five in appallingly crowded conditions, which even precluded the comfort of a fire in winter.[149] It is also true that in 1833/4 only two factories in the whole of Lancashire (one of them being the firm of Horrocks Crewdson, a firm long associated with Simpsons) met with the approval of the factory inspectors.[150] Nevertheless, the Factory Acts were enforced and conditions constantly improved. In fact, no criticisms of this kind could be levelled against the wire drawing industry. Mr. Walmsley of Simpsons speaks of them being able to provide much better and cleaner working conditions than in the cotton mills, and of his remembrance of the older employees talking of the work there as being inviting because it kept them from the noise of the mills.[151] The really rather dreadful immoralities associated with mill work[152] were obviously also avoided in the smaller and more efficiently supervised factories of the wire drawing trade. Wages, too, were better, not necessarily than in the mills where they were comparatively high, but incomparably better than in the cottage industries. In the 1860's a girl of eight in the Buckinghamshire/Oxfordshire lace-making area might make 1s. 6d. to 2s. 6d. per week for a nine-hour day. A girl of 13 of moderate ability working a 10 hour day might earn 2s. 6d. to 3s. 0d.[153] Workers in factories earned far more. Spinners on fine counts earned 40s. 0 d. in the 1840's. Power loom weavers from 10s. 0d. to 16s. 0d. in 1846, 15s. 0d.–18s. 0d. per week by the 1880's.[154] There are no figures for the gold and silver wire-drawers but they will not have been significantly less.

Indeed the gold and silver wire-drawers seem to have had a remarkable history of happy relations with their work-people. Simpsons' first employee, Martha Riley, stayed with the firm for 44 years, all her working life, and when he died Isaac Simpson left her an annuity of £20 in his will.[155] Her nieces, Ada and Ivy Fielding, later worked for the firm until their retirement.[156] Firms engaged in the trade took on many people for their entire working lives and employed whole generations of families. At Simpsons Annie Kaupp worked for over 70 years, Isabella Ellen Boast for 58 years, John Barnes for 43 years,[157] Henry Preston for 50, his two sons Daniel Preston[158] and Fred Preston[159] followed him into the business: their engineers A. E. Buck, Senior and Junior, each served 50 years. John Sharps, who employed seven males and 20 females, had many members of staff who were employed for over forty years.[160] As we have seen at Benton and Johnson, the employees of Barrett and Corney were not made redundant but were absorbed into the business.

All this was only possible because the businesses were steady and well run and the supply of work was continuous. Expanding markets within the British Empire made much of this possible and the contraction of the trade at the beginning of the century had also helped because it had left sufficient work for the remaining firms. Even in the terrible times of the cotton famine in the 1870's the wire-drawing firms were free from the industrial disturbances of their near neighbours. J. and A. Leigh, the cotton spinners in Preston, had to call out the Lancers to protect their house from being burnt by the enraged strikers but the wire-drawing firms of Simpson, Tootell, and John Sharp were left unmolested.[161]

One of the reasons for these good relations was that the wire-drawing firms continued to be family run and maintained. The Simpson family, even when Stephen Simpson died in 1891 and the firm had to be handed over to trustees, did not relinquish its family connection. Indeed the trusteeship was only necessary because Stephen Simpson had invested so much capital in the business that his legacies could only be paid from the profits. Within only six years the returns on the investment were sufficient for all the legacies to be paid and the business reverted to Stephen's heirs.[162] Two great, great-grandsons of Isaac Simpson are still in the firm. Jeremy John Kentish-Barnes A.C.A. is on the board of the main company and William Stephen Kentish-Barnes, having entered the firm on the shop floor, is now a director of the London subsidiary, Benton and Johnson.[163] There was a Benton at Benton and Johnson until 1958[164] and there is still a Johnson, although the firm is now part of the Simpson group. Henry Johnson and George Benton married sisters.[165] Isaac Simpson's first agent in Glasgow was his sister.[166] When George Benton died his wife carried on alone until Henry Johnson joined her.[167] John Sharp continued to be family-owned until it was bought by Simpsons.[168] At G. L. Tootell, Edward Leigh, who bought the firm from George Leigh Tootell in 1901, was succeeded on his death by his son Edward Howard Leigh.[169]

Besides very happy relationships inside the firms, the trade was also characterised by very happy inter-firm contacts. The Preston wire-drawing firms even had a joint yearly outing about which many anecdotes are still told.[170] There was a particularly close friendship between Leslie Johnson the father of the three present members of the Gold and Silver Wyre Drawers and William Chadderton the chairman and managing director of Stephen Simpson.[171] In the case of Benton and Johnson the good relationships extended to foreign firms. When Sidney Johnson was brought into Benton and Johnson by his father, the third Henry William, he went to a firm in Lyons to learn about the tinsel trade. The connection with this city continues in a friendly way to this day.[172]

The good relations were the more remarkable in that competition was extremely fierce and from the 1920's it was set against a background of economic slump and a contracting market. The German blockade hit the 'Lancashire Trade' during the First World War and when India started making cloth and using a gilt stamp as a heading it got worse and worse.[173] The 'Lancashire Trade' disappeared altogether, at John Sharp's by 1939,[174] and at Tootell's a last few orders were placed in the 1960's.[175] The two Lancashire firms of E. and W. G. Makinson of the Wellfield Works, Preston, and Alexander Grimshaw of Miles Platting, Manchester, went out of business in the 1930's.[176] John Sharp's made its first loss ever in 1931.[177] The firm of Stantons in the south ceased trading in the 1920's.[178]

The Preston firms which remained had to look to other markets in order to survive. Stephen Simpson had started a hand embroidery department as early as 1898 and was making machine embroidery and epaulettes by 1902.[179] The firm had been manufacturing the materials for embroidery from the time they ceased trading in partnership with Johnson's in the 1870's.[180] Lace-making had been started in 1875 and in that year Simpson's acquired its first contract for the supply of gold lace to the Army.[181] In 1878 the first lace to be woven by steam power was woven by Bertha Chadderton at the works in Preston.[182] Then in the 'twenties the other two firms turned over their machines to making embroidery materials. Sales to this trade are reckoned by Mr. Leigh, the owner of G. H. L. Tootell,[183] and Mr. Fitch, the managing director[184] of John Sharp, to have saved their firms. Tootell's had given up actual wire-drawing by 1908 and turned to the manufacture of braid, plated linen thread for measuring tapes, and threads and cords for the decorative and packaging trades.[185]

The major customers for embroidery threads and wires were Toye's the Masonic suppliers, Hobson's, the military outfitters, and Gieves, the Naval tailors. Neither firm was slow to exploit so favourable a situation and competition was fierce. Toye's were particularly renowned for the briskness of their bargaining.[186]

The firms were not only competitive in the market but also forward looking in their investment policies, particularly by constantly improving their machinery. G. H. L. Tootell changed from steam to gas engines in 1906 and to electricity in 1933. It changed from hand to automatic flatting in the 1920's.[187] Sharp's never adopted automatic flatting but were the only company to make pearl purl by machine. When E. and W. G. Makinson Ltd. of the Wellfields Works, Preston, ceased trading in the 1930's Sharp's invested in some of their machinery.

Working conditions were also constantly improving, not only because the new machinery was cleaner and quieter but because hours were shorter and wages increased. Sharp's first introduced an annual paid holiday in 1935, which caused some annoyance to their competitors when it was announced in the local paper.[188]

In the south, Benton and Johnson under the very able guidance of the third Henry William diversified within the family. When Henry William inherited his father's firm he amalgamated it with Benton and Johnson, taking seven-eighths of the capital and leaving Mrs. Benton with one eighth for her son, George. He put his two sons, Herbert William and Sidney, into Benton and Johnson. His third son, Cyril, joined Stillwells, who were manufacturers of braids, laces and embroidery. When Stanton's ceased trading in the 1920's Benton and Johnson bought the stock.[189]

In all this, however, Simpson's were in a much more viable position than the other firms not only because they had started their own lace-making and embroidery departments long before the other firms considered diversifying but because they had started their own hand embroidery retailing side. Today Stephen Simpson have their own Masonic department. The Company also further diversified by turning its machinery over to the making of telephone wires and strings for musical instruments. It also started to electroplate gold and silver on to copper wire as well as using the older methods.[190] Simpson's agents were widespread, indeed. In 1929 they had representatives in England, Wales, Scotland, Ireland, Canada, Australia, Egypt and India.[191] The Company was easily the most formidable. In an ever-contracting market with fierce competition from Pakistan in the 1950's[192] and under post-war pressures from taxation and high interest rates, monopolisation was not only inevitable but sensible.

John Sharp's and Benton and Johnson joined the Simpson Group in the 1960s,[193] and G. L. Tootell closed down in 1971.[194] These mergers were very much in accordance with the gentle manners of the trade. John Sharp's staff was taken into Simpson's and Albert Redman, John Sharp's foreman, is the present foreman of Simpson's bar shed.[195] Even Tootell's has not entirely ceased its contact with the trade for when Mr. Leigh closed the firm down he sold some of his braiding machinery to Simpson's.

It would be wrong to end on what must be a sad note. The trade today has of course contracted but it is still important. The products of the wire-maker's skill are not only extensively used by Simpson's in their own workshops and retailed by them through their mercantile and masonic departments, and their London firm of Benton and Johnson, but they also supply other embroiderers and retailers. Foremost among these are Toye's and the Royal School of Needlework.[196] Toye's need no explanation here. The Royal School uses gold and silver wire extensively for regimental colours and uniforms, for ecclesiastical embroidery and for repair work. Incidentally, the Ministry of Defence is extremely exigent about the quality of the needlework it will accept and sends an officer to inspect and count the number of stitches in each piece of work. He does this even in that minor miracle of the embroiderer's skill, the regimental colour. These colours must be the same on both sides and so both sides are embroidered at once. Repair work also calls for large numbers of gold and silver threads; for example, the exquisite blackwork of the 16th century relies entirely for its effect and delicacy on the use of silver thread.[197]

In the export market the only major competitor to Britain in Europe is France which has a gold and silver wire-making industry centred round the silk-making district of Lyons. Britain actually exports to India, since the Indians find it cheaper to buy British products than manufacture their own. Benton and Johnson also export to Australia, New Zealand, Malta, Canada, Nigeria, S. Africa, Bahrein and Pakistan.[198]

The industry is small and monopolised. Simpson's themselves would not find it profitable to draw gold and silver wire were it not for their own large embroidery and weaving sections, and the fact that they also make telephone cables and strings for musical instruments.[199] Nevertheless it commands a more extensive market than Alderman Garroway ever dreamed of, and can at least boast, unlike that city worthy, that goods of inferior quality are never sold and least of all to Russia.[200] In the end it is enough to say that the industry survives and that what it does is well done.

The bobbin label of Stephen Simpson, c. 1831

VII

What the Company is doing in the 20th Century

TO THOSE who have lived through it, the 20th century has seemed one of the most disastrous in the country's history. Two World Wars and economic depression have been followed by post-war austerity; economic and moral uncertainty at home; and falling prestige abroad. Throughout all this the City of London has supported the morale of its citizens. St. Paul's became during the war a symbol of the country's determination to survive. London Bridge, re-erected in an American desert, is a monument to a sense of business enterprise worthy of Thomas Violet himself.

The Company of Gold and Silver Wyre-Drawers has shared and suffered in all the tumultuous events of the century and despite all has increased its strength and enlarged and concentrated its charitable pre-occupations. More than anything it has been intent on preserving and strengthening its links with the trade.

The century does not seem to have started well for the Gold and Silver Wyre-Drawers. At all events that is, according to the opinion of the Committee set up in 1926 for the reorganisation of the Company, which complained of a lack of status and vitality.[1] The Court Book for this period is lost but the sad views of the Committee are not apparent from the surviving cash book. The Company seems to have been very jolly. There was a ball in 1902 provided by J. Lyons and Co. costing £219 10s. 0d.,[2] and a dinner in 1903 costing £115 14s. 8d.[3] The Company ate its first Ring and Brymer dinner at Clothworkers' Hall in 1909. This cost rather more: £161 6s. 0d. for Ring and Brymer, and 15 guineas for the loan of the Hall.[4] There was a dinner in 1911,[5] and banquets in 1912,[6] and 1913,[7] at De Keyser's Hotel. These last cost £247 17s. 6d. and £236 1s. 3d.

The more serious duties of the Company do not appear to have been neglected. The Barnsbury property was surveyed in 1904[8] and the purchase of ground rents at Westcliffe on Sea was completed in 1906.[9] During the war the Gold and Silver Wyre-Drawers gave generously from their pitiably small funds. They gave £105 to the Prince of Wales fund[10] and numerous small sums to other war charities[11] even down to five guineas to Lady Parkington for the Montenegrin Red Cross of all unlikely things.[12] Investments were all made in War stock.[13] At the end of the War they were quick to join the City rejoicing and in 1918 contributed £26 5s. 0d. towards the testimonial to President Hoover of the United States.[14] In the midst of the War in 1915/16 the Charitable fund, which had been started in 1907 for members and their dependants, received its first investment.[15] The fund was also fully discussed.

Even if the committee's gloom were justified, on its own evidence the Company was beginning to revive by 1921.[16] This revival is attributed to the activity of a new Clerk appointed in 1919.[17] He was Athro Charles Knight J.P., F.S.A., C.C. and was one of the many clerks from John Borrett downwards to whom the Company owes so much. In the first five years he increased the Poor Fund by investing wisely, and improved the Company's general financial position by encouraging an influx of new members both into the Company and onto the Court.[18] He negotiated the increases in the livery in 1926,[19] and 1943[20] and of fees in 1935.[21] During his tenure of office the Company increased its status and held secure its contacts with the Trade.

The Company was not ungrateful. In 1926 it raised his honorarium from £50 to £75 with the promise that if the livery were increased it should be raised to £100.[22] In 1945 the Court granted him the honorary freedom and livery and a subscription of £176 8s. 0d. which was used to buy a portrait of his wife.[23] When he retired in 1955 another present of £135 14s 2d. was given him by a subscription from the livery at large.[24] The first increase was made with a comment from the Court that 'It is considered rather a privilege among practising solicitors to secure an appointment of this nature'.[25] Of course 'the privilege' was to be accounted as part of Mr. Knight's honorarium. He did not have another increase in salary until 1953[26] when the honorarium which had been increased twice, in 1926 from £50 to £75 and then again to £100,[27] was doubled.[28]

The number of the livery was raised from 150 to 200 with the agreement of the Court of Aldermen in October 1926 at a cost of £20.[29] The fees were increased as follows: redemption from £39 5s. 6d. to 50 guineas and election to the Court to the same. This certainly improved the Company's financial position. It probably also improved its morale for in 1927 it gave the first Public Exhibition devoted entirely to the craft.

The exhibition was held at Stationers' Hall from Wednesday, 29 June until Friday 1 July. The exhibits in the main hall showed the various stages of gold and silver wire-drawing from the silver in block or granulated form, through the cast bar, to wire, the fineness of 3500 yards per ounce. The exhibition continued with the methods of spinning gold and silver thread, flatting gold and silver wires, and drawing gold and silver fine wire. There was also a hand-purling spindle making pearl-purl, a hand-bullion spindle and a hand-twisting wheel, a Jacquard loom for lace-making and a loom for weaving gold, silver and silk fringes by hand. Practical demonstrations were given by embroideresses making trumpet banners, belts, badges, epaulettes, aiguillettes, tassels and sword knots. In the adjoining hall were examples of the embroiderer's art with gold and silver wire, ranging from a waistcoat made for Henry William Johnson (Master 1840) by his work people on the occasion of his wedding, to a section of a dress aiguillette presented by Edward VII to his nephew Kaiser Wilhelm II. There was also a gold girdle made for Queen Victoria's native tutor in Hindustani.[30]

On the second day Her Majesty Queen Mary visited the exhibition.[31] She later accepted a copy of the brochure presented by the Company for which she sent thanks.[32]

The Committee members responsible for this highly successful venture were A.

Rochester Brown, George Benton, Colonel Stephen Simpson, A. W. Smith, C. D. Stillwell and Lt-Colonel Cart de Lafontaine. A large proportion of them were members of the trade and if Colonel de Lafontaine was not a member of the trade he was none the less indispensable, since only he had been able to get the hall arranged for the working machinery.[33]

The exhibition was opened by an Honorary Liveryman, the Rt. Hon. Sir Philip Cunliffe Lister M.P., then President of the Board of Trade. When the exhibition was over Colonel Simpson gave the banner of the Company's Arms, which had been made for it, to the Company.[34] The success of all this is proved by the fact that when the Royal Academy and the Royal Society of Arts proposed an exhibition in 1933 they asked the Company to be represented on the Committee.[35]

In the inter-war years the Gold and Silver Wyre-Drawers continued to receive additions to their plate and regalia. George Benton, long connected with the Company and the trade, gave a loving cup in 1926.[36] Robert Cuthbertson, master in 1916, gave a hundred pounds in his will for a piece of plate in 1925; a cup and cover was duly purchased.[37] The cover is surmounted by the Company's Arms set with green agates and moonstones.[38] Lady Dron also gave a silver two-handled cup.[39] Mr. Rochester Brown presented a silver inkstand with the arms in gold and enamel in 1931.[40] Mr. Sendell gave a £100 in 1933 for a piece of plate.[41] Mrs. Walker gave an épergne in 1936.[42] The High Sheriff of Durham gave a length of the first transatlantic cable.[43] Colonel de Lafontaine gave a copy of the original proclamation of James I dated 30 March 1621[44] and Sir Percy Vincent a broadsheet dated 1712.[45] Both these last were deposited at Guildhall. The Master in 1939, Norman L. Ball J.P., bought the Beadle a new hat.[46]

Celebrations also continued. The Company had a decorative car in the Lord Mayor's Show in 1928. This was arranged by members of the craft and was not to cost more than £50.[47] The Company also took part in the processions in 1930,[48] 1932 and in 1935. In 1932 the Court provided two carriages and banners[49] and in 1935, three carriages, a corps of commissionaires, a band and banners.[50] The banners by this time were feeling the effects of long service and had to be repaired at a cost of £23 19s. 6d. in the following year, 1936[51]. Civic gloves were given to Sir Percy Vincent in 1936.[52] Banquets were held each year, quite often by this time in the Halls of other Livery Companies. In 1931 the Gold and Silver Wyre-Drawers went to Grocers' Hall,[53] in 1933 to Salters' Hall[54] and in 1937 to Merchant Taylors' Hall.[55]

All the time the standing of the Company and of its members was rising. In 1930 three members of the Court, Sir Harold Downer LL.B., Sir Maurice Jenks Bt., LL.D., F.C.A. and Sir Percy Vincent were all Aldermen.[56] Besides the Clerk, W. J. Trice (Master 1925), Fred Gillet (Master 1927), A. Stanley Bell, (Master 1930) and A. E. Watts F.C.A. (Master 1933) were all Common Councillors.[57] Colonel Stephen Simpson, M.A., T.D., Master in 1932, was a Deputy-Lieutenant for the County Palatine of Lancaster.[58] Sir Henry Curtis Bennett, K.C., was chairman of the Essex Quarter Sessions.[59] J. D. Cassells became a High Court Judge.[60] An honorary freeman, Sir Philip Cunliffe Lister (later Earl of Swinton) was President of the Board of Trade,[61] and a mere liveryman, Geoffrey Nevall, was High Sheriff of Durham.[62]

At the same time the Court continued to cherish its contacts with the trade: not only by giving exhibitions but also by keeping the number of members who were active in the trade as large as possible. It always gave them precedence for admission to the Court. In 1937 a committee was formed to examine the possibility of granting freedoms to skilled operatives.[63] In 1939 two wire drawers and wire rope manufacturers from the Rees family, of Grave Works, Whitchurch, Glamorgan, were admitted by redemption.[64]

The Company was always trying to increase its financial stability. The fines were again raised in 1935 when the fine for freedom by patrimony, and servitude and for steward was put up to £42 18s. od.[65] With the knowledge that much of the wealth of the older city companies had come from property investment the Court perhaps misguidedly at this particular time decided to do the same and invested in ground rents. The Mortlake property was sold in 1931, but the resulting £2,000 was re-invested in properties in Barnet,[66] as was the War stock which was redeemed in 1932.[67] However some of this process was reversed in 1938 when the Barnsbury Terrace property was sold and, with war looming near, the Court again invested in War Stock.[68] The Assistants were competent landlords and repaired the properties and exacted proper behaviour from their tenants.[69] The Southend and Mortlake properties gave some trouble in 1930 but it was quickly over.[70]

The Company's principal charitable donations at this time came from the Mrs. Christian Russell Fund for widows and the Charitable Fund set up in 1907 and formalized in 1915/16 for members and their dependents. These funds, although small, were of real use in the 'thirties when unemployment was rife and widows and spinsters numerous. The Court Book records the following sums given to dependents: £5 to Miss Rooke 'as usual', £13 per annum to Miss Martha Coles, and £1 monthly each to Miss White and Miss Edwards.[71] All of these were Mrs. Christian Russell beneficiaries. Grants of £10 and £15 2s. 8d. with £21 5s. od. for rent and rates were made to a liveryman in 1931[72] and a further allowance of two guineas for 10 weeks made to another member of the livery in the same year.[73] A most generous donation of £250 in 1933 by George Ernest Sendell greatly helped the Poor Fund.[74]

The Poor Fund was also to be used for city charities or ones under the aegis of the Lord Mayor and various sums were dispensed to such objects. There was a donation of three guineas to the restoration of Bow Church,[75] 25 guineas to London University,[76] 10 guineas towards the Lord Mayor's appeal for the Prince of Wales thank offering fund in 1935,[77] and 20 guineas to the memorial for George V.[78]

These were sad and apprehensive times. Families were recovering from one war and under the shadow of another. The minds of the members were forever turning, even amid the jollifications and in the middle of the increased status and prosperity of the Company, to the events around them. Even at the opening of the 1927 Exhibition a troubled note was struck by the Master, Fred Gillet's speech, which commented on the diminishing number of skilled workmen.[79] In the circumstances of the depression the Court had to be careful and an invitation to exhibit the craft with the Coronation regalia at South Kensington in 1937 had to be declined as 'not desirable'.[80] Displays of wealth even such artistic ones as those made by the wire-drawers were not possible when trade was so bad. In small ways there were reminders of the great loss of men in the first war and the many families who had lost sons. Colonel H. P. L. de Lafontaine O.B.E., T.D., F.R.I.B.A., was not just the indispensible arranger of Halls for machinery, in his profession he was the principal officer of the War Graves Commission.[81]

The Court Minutes first adumbrate the second world war in July 1938, when the Barnsbury property proceeds were invested in War Stock and a proposal to adopt the First Anti-Aircraft Division R.A.S.C., T.A. was declined.[82] Thereafter things escalated. Norman L. Ball, J.P. (Master 1938) was appointed Colonel of the First Anti-Aircraft Division in 1939.[83] The Company gave 50 guineas to the Red Cross and the St. John's War organisation in the same year,[84] and in the dread of air raids and because of the difficulties of the 'Blackout' abandoned all idea of a banquet. Three luncheons were given to the livery instead.[85] Food shortages were already feared and the Master entertained the Court to light refreshments.[86] By 1941 the apprentices being made free were already serving in the forces.[87]

As the war continued the Gold and Silver Wyre-Drawers, with the rest of the City, had losses both personal and material. One of the Company's most interesting pieces of plate commemorates one of the former. It is a silver tankard which was owned and used in turn by E. Stillwell (Master in 1827), E. S. Stillwell (Master in 1856) and C. D. Stillwell (Master in 1939 and 1940). It was given by Mrs. E. W. D. Stillwell in 1943 in memory of her husband Major Eric William Digby Stillwell, the son of C. D. Stillwell, and the grandson and great-grandson of E. S. and E. Stillwell. Major Stillwell was a liveryman. He was killed in action in Egypt.[88]

In the air attacks of 29–30 December 1940 the premises of C. D. Stillwell, and C. W. Palmer were destroyed and the premises of other members of the Court were badly damaged.[89] The Clerk's offices at 33 Walbrook were destroyed on 10 May 1941 and with them some of the Company's property.[90] Fortunately, the older archives were safe; Mr Knight had deposited them at Guildhall on 3 November 1922,[91] but some documents of title and some of the accounts were lost, as were a freedom stamp book, 300 brochures of the Company's history, some gowns, a cigar cabinet, a framed coat of arms, and the Beadle's new hat. A silver seal on the first insurance list was recovered from the wreckage. It was cleaned, boxed, and embellished with an ivory handle by Past Master Mr. Hicklenton in 1956.[92]

The Company did what it could for the war effort but this was naturally not a great deal. Besides contributions to the Lord Mayor's Air Relief Fund, the Lord Mayor's Comforts League[93] and the Red Cross and St. John War institution,[94] it put all possible savings into War Stock. £200 was added to the original 1938 investment in 1943 and was put in 3% Defence Bonds.[95] £500 was invested in 2½% National War Bonds 1952/4 in 1944 as a gesture of solidarity in 'Salute the Soldier' week.[96] As late as 1946 the Company put £800 and £200 in 3% Defence Bonds.[97]

The Court's real contribution was its determination to preserve morale. Companies who lost their halls were sent letters of condolence, those who had escaped for the time being letters of congratulation.[98] Innholders' Hall where the Company had been holding courts since 1924[99] escaped destruction even in the bad attacks of 1941.[100] Evening entertainments were not popular because of the Blitz and the blackout, neither were 'men only' functions when so many were being posted overseas, so the Court instituted livery luncheons with dances. The first of these was held at the Connaught Rooms in April 1942[101] and was so much enjoyed that the Company held them every year afterwards. An amendment that the dance should be discontinued and a luncheon only held was lost out of hand in 1944.[102]

Best of all, the Company continued to plan and behave as if the war were a temporary inconvenience which should not be allowed to interfere with the proper running of its own affairs. In 1939 a committee was formed in an attempt to increase the charitable funds and put them on a legal footing. The outbreak of war caused a temporary setback since it was thought unsuitable to make an appeal to the livery at such a time,[103] but by July 1940 a new trust fund had been fairly launched.[104] It attracted seven-year covenants from J. H. Morton,[105] C. Digby Stillwell and L. W. Johnson among others. These new contributions were immediately invested in $3\frac{1}{2}\%$ War Stock.[106] Unfortunately, some of the earlier funds had been invested before the war in Japanese sterling loan 1907. When Japan came into the war the stock was temporarily worthless and did not recover until well after the cessation of hostilities.[107] The Stock was sold in 1959[108] and the proceeds were invested in 5% Australian Commonwealth Stock.[109]

By 1943 the Company was managing to hold its place so well that a petition was made for another increase from 200 to 250 in the livery. The fines were to remain the same, and six new liverymen only were to be admitted at each Court meeting unless three-quarters of the Court agreed otherwise.[110] The Court of Aldermen in customary form granted the increase on condition that the Company did not exceed the new number.[111]

In other ways, too, the Gold and Silver Wyre-Drawers looked forward. As early as 1942 Colonel Cart de Lafontaine was putting forward proposals for buying a site for a Hall which could be used by all the companies who had none of their own.[112] When the war did end the Court had been expecting it so long that it passed unremarked. It did not even, like the deaths of George VI[113] and Queen Mary[114], merit a mention in the minutes. There was, however, a banquet for the first time since 1939. It was held at Grocers' Hall.[115] A luncheon and dance at the Connaught Rooms was paid for by the liverymen themselves.[116]

The post-war period posed many problems, not least one of the Court's own making. The increase in the livery and the return of liverymen who had been clothed at the beginning of the war but had since been overseas meant that many members of the Company were not well known to the Court. This was particularly embarrassing when liverymen came forward for election to the Court and the Assistants had to enquire amongst themselves as to their qualifications and virtues. Things were so bad that many were hardly known to the Clerk. When it was proposed to give a testimonial to Mr. Knight for his 25-years service in 1945, the Assistants thought it inappropriate to ask the livery to contribute, since 94 of the liverymen had met him only once.[117]

Fortunately, the Court was very alive to the difficulty and made every effort to remedy the situation. Livery luncheons were started which, owing to the shortages of funds, had to be paid for by the livery themselves. However two luncheons were held, one in 1946 at Apothecaries' Hall[118] and one in 1947 at Innholders'. The latter luncheon cost 30s. 0d. a head[119] which was quite a lot then, but seems scarcely believable now. Measures were also taken to inform new liverymen of their commitments, and in 1948 the Court passed a resolution that candidates for the livery must be interviewed and told their financial obligations.[120]

The Court was much helped in this difficulty by the fact that a Masonic Lodge had been formed in 1944.[121] The Lodge provided more frequent opportunities for liverymen to meet and on a different basis from that of the Company. It was particularly useful in promoting and establishing friendly contacts within the Company. The Court thought it very well worthwhile to mention the Lodge in the next list of members[122] and its affairs are now regularly reported in the Master's yearly report to the livery.[123]

The Court also grasped the opportunity to enter a team for the Livery Companies' Golfing Society and since 1946 has subscribed regularly to that Society.[124] In 1952 the Gold and Silver Wyre-Drawers team came eighth in the Prince Arthur of Connaught Golf Competition[125] and a regular golfing society, now also always mentioned in the Master's Report, was founded in 1961.[126]

The further increase of the livery from 250 to 350 in 1956,[127] was attended by similar difficulties and greatly increased the administrative burden for the Clerk. In 1958 it became necessary to formalise the procedure whereby the Assistants addressed the Court on the qualifications of their candidates when elections to the Court were being made.[128] Altogether though, these slight matters, with the especial help of the two societies, the greater opportunities for meeting provided by the generosity of the Masters of recent years and the care and trouble of the administrative officials. have been successfully overcome.

Other potentially awkward matters were settled as well. In 1961 the Court passed a resolution that all Assistants should make an undertaking on election to resign if unable to undertake the duties of their office.[129] A resolution that Past Masters should be fined 5s. 0d. for the Poor Box if they came without their badge was obviously of a more playful nature, since the Assistant proposing this measure, Past Master, Sir George Wilkinson, was himself the offender on that particular occasion and immediately paid the fine.[130]

In the immediate post-war years the Company played with a long cherished dream, the acquisition of a hall. This scheme was pressed by Colonel Cart de Lafontaine, who was himself an architect. He worked very hard to turn this castle in the air into real bricks and mortar. From 1948–1954 the venture looked as if it might really succeed.[131] Colonel Cart de Lafontaine prepared sketch plans at his own cost of a Hall and offices which he calculated would cost £168,000 to build. It was estimated that these offices would bring in a rent of £16,000 per annum, and as this seemed sound to the Court, notice was given to Colonel Cart de Lafontaine to provide a detailed financial statement and to find a site.[132] In 1952 the Committee considering the matter were empowered to buy the option on a site in the city for not more than £25.[133] The detailed scheme was prepared and considered and £25 was voted for a further legal opinion in the same year.[134] Alas, after all this, the matter was found to be impracticable and the affair was abandoned in 1954.[135] The idea of building a hall was revived for a time during the Mastership of Bernard Thorpe in 1966[136] but again came to nothing. The Company's banners, worn out at last, ended their days at Sion College, the home of the City Livery Club.[137]

The Gold and Silver Wyre-Drawers may not have built a Hall but they continued to invest in property. One of the houses at Barnet, 39 Western Way was badly damaged by fire in 1958,[138] but it was insured, and was rebuilt by October in the same year.[139] It is pleasant to see that the members of the Court behaved as good landlords do and remitted the ground rent during non-occupation. The Assistants agreed to the erection of a garage on the Barnet property in 1961.[140]

Since the war the Company has continued to be fortunate in the generosity of its members. It had a particularly charming present in 1947 when Michael Gerder presented a representation of the Coat of Arms worked in gold, silver and platinum on glass. This was alas broken and never replaced.[141] In 1951 Stanley Bell gave a silver bowl, a reproduction of one of four originals presented to the Mansion House to mark the mayoralty of Sir John Emaer in 1801.[142] Herbert Toye repaired the banners,[143] had the first Warden's badge enamelled to match the other badges[144] and gave a silver wire card case which had been in his family for generations.[145] Bernard Thorpe gave an illuminated show case to hold it.[146] New livery gowns were presented by the Master, Herbert Toye, and Wardens Frederick A. Grant J.P., George F. Baker and Dennis Johnson in 1961. Other Badges were also given by J. W. Perry and H. G. D. Toye. Andrew Johnson gave a dress chain for the Master's badge.[147] Bernard Thorpe presented an exemplar of gold wire woven into designs and framed, in 1967. Philip Cresswell, when he resigned as Clerk in 1974, gave a fine silver gilt goblet for the use of the Master. Leslie Boyd and Norman Harding donated a gown, laced with silver wire, in 1970 for the Clerk to wear. The Company has had stranger offerings. Albert Bernays, a liveryman, gave 1,300 Norwich Crematorium Ltd. ordinary shares, the interest of which was to pay for an annual invitation to a Banquet or Court luncheon to a visitor from the United States or the Commonwealth.[148] The presentation of crematorium shares for providing dinners was a favourite joke of Mr Bernays. He made a similar donation to the Vintners' Company to provide funds for what is now known as the Gale and Bernays dinner.[149] The Court of the Gold and Silver Wyre-Drawers accepted his offer with insouciance and gratitude.

In the last year the Company has had a very well considered donation. Mr. Warden Ross-Goobey and Mrs. Cole have subscribed the money for the fee to the College of Arms for regularising and registering the Arms.[150] Mrs. Cole gave the scale fee for the supporters in memory of her husband Harold Cole. Mr. Cole was a liveryman, one of the supporters is a liveryman, and most generously Mrs. Cole felt this to be most appropriate.[151] The patent was granted and signed and sealed by the Kings of Arms in 1975.[152] The Arms are now correctly blazoned; Azure on a Chevron Or between in chief two Engrossing Blocks Or and in base two points in saltire Argent a Drawing Iron between two Rings Sable and for the Crest, on a Wreath Or and Azure, Two arms embowed vested Gules cuffed Argent holding in the hands proper a Copper Gold, and for Supporters, on the dexter side a Carib Indian proper crowned with an Ancient Crown Or vested about the waist with feathers pendent alternately Argent and Gules holding over the shoulder a Bar of Silver proper and on the sinister side a Liveryman of the Company of the mid 18th. Century having over the outer arm a coil of drawn Wire all proper.

The Patent recites that the Art and Mystery of the Gold and Silver Wyre Drawers had been of long continuance in London and had received a Royal Charter of Incorporation bearing date the 16th day of June 1693 and thereafter had used upon its Common Seal certain Arms and Crest together with Supporters 'for more than two hundred years without the same having been duly registered at the College of Arms as of right pertaining to the said Company'.

The Patent also refers to the Company's desire to have the said Armorial Ensigns 'duly confirmed and granted with lawful authority' in consequence of which the Earl Marshal issued his Warrant on 22nd. November 1974, authorizing and directing the Kings of Arms to grant and confirm such Armorial Ensigns accordingly.

The rationale of the Arms is to be sought in the combination of the tools of the trade and implements used by members of the Company and at the Company's request the position of some of these has been varied from that which they occupied in the assumed Arms, viz: instead of two 'Coppers' in the chief of the Shield there is now a pair of Engrossing Blocks, and in the Crest such a Block has been replaced by a Copper.

The Supporters have been interpreted variously in the past, but the Patent settles their identity as respectively a Carib Indian and a Liveryman of the Company carrying a coil of drawn wire on his outer arm.

The matter of the grant of Arms was conducted at the College of Arms by Windsor Herald, A. Colin Cole, son of the former Liveryman.[153]

The Company has continued to be well served by its officers. When Athro Charles Knight retired in 1955 he was succeeded by Philip H. Cresswell, C.C., a liveryman of 19 years standing, who had already served three years as an Assistant. He served as Clerk for a further 19 years until 1974, except for the year 1967 when he undertook the hardly less onerous office of Master. He is still a member of the Court.[154] In latter years and in 1967 during his years as Master, Mr. Cresswell was assisted in his office by Norman Harding, C.C. Mr. Harding is also a member of the Court and continues to act as assistant to the new Clerk, David Reid, F.C.A.[155] Mr. Rawles, who had been Beadle for 25 years, retired in 1956[156] and Mr. Baldock served in his stead[157] until 1976, when he was succeeded by Mr. H. F. Moore. The Court made Mr. Rawles a present of 35 guineas and gave Mr. Baldock a gold watch in recognition of their services.

Financially, the Company has managed to maintain its position, in spite of inflation and rising costs everywhere. It has made such shrewd financial investments as lay within its means[158] and has been helped by the new livery grant which besides permitting more clothings also put up the fees.

One very sad economy has been made. The cost of the annual livery banquet rose out of all proportion to the other expenditure of the Company, and liverymen now pay for their own dinners. The Court were quite rightly reluctant to come to this decision.[159] The banquet is the centre of the livery's activity and the Company was formed first to be a trade fraternity with the intention of fostering good fellowship, long before it acquired any charitable duties. Costs have now risen so high that fewer liverymen can afford to attend and this in the future may bring its own problems.[160]

Luckily there has been a great increase in other livery functions in recent years which should counter some of the ill effects.[161]

The use of the Mansion House for the annual banquet has become almost traditional over the years, but it is not a right and is not invariable. Since the war the banquet has been held elsewhere six times, at Grocers' Hall in 1945[162] and 1958[163] at Tallow Chandlers' Hall in 1948,[164] at the Savoy Hotel in 1949,[165] at Guildhall in 1961[166] and 1966.[167] Guildhall was used on the two latter occasions in preference to Mansion House, because of the large number of liverymen and their guests who wished to attend. Herbert G. D. Toye was Master in 1961; Bernard Thorpe in 1966.[168] On at least one occasion, 1958, the Company did not use the Mansion House because the Lord Mayor would not lend it. The Court of Aldermen made a decision in that year that the Mansion House was not to be used for Livery Banquets, and despite a further application by another past Lord Mayor, Sir George Wilkinson, the Mansion House was denied. This even though the application was made on the advice of Sir Denys Lowson who was soon himself to be Lord Mayor. The Gold and Silver Wyre-Drawers blessed the clerk's foresight in having already booked Grocers' Hall.[169] The following year they came near to disaster. The Livery Banquet was held at Mansion House but the guests were so late in leaving that members of the Court were concerned that unless proceedings were curtailed the Mansion House would not be available in future.[170] Of course they were, and the livery continues to be grateful for the Lord Mayor's generosity, who not only lends his house but also honours them by coming to the banquet.

In recent years the Masters have not only been distinguished men, Herbert Toye was Sheriff in 1966 and Ralph Hedderwick has been both Sheriff and Master of the Company in 1976, they have also been men of many pursuits and wide interests. The livery has greatly benefited from this and has enjoyed the variety of venues for cocktail parties and the organisation of other activities. In 1966 during Bernard Thorpe's year of office, a cocktail party was held at the Baltic exchange.[171] In 1967 when Philip Cresswell was Master there was a reception and cocktail party at the Central Criminal Court, Old Bailey.[172] In 1968, when Mr. George Perkins was Master, the livery went to the Mermaid Theatre to a performance of *Hadrian VII*.[173] In 1969 during Leslie Boyd's tenure of office the Company went to the Old Bailey again.[174] In 1970 the year of Frank Smith the Company went again to the Mermaid Theatre and to Armoury House. In 1972 the Gold and Silver Wyre-Drawers held fête unlimited. There were cocktail parties on H.M.S. Belfast and at the House of Lords, a buffet supper at the Mermaid Theatre and a private visit to the Tutankhamun exhibition. The Master's dinner, which had been instituted by Frank Smith, was held that year by Clifford Jeapes in the Disraeli Room of the Junior Carlton Club and a cocktail party for the Court and their ladies on the Martini Terrace of New Zealand House.[175] The year following, when Douglas Dunstan was Master, was scarcely less festive. There were cocktail parties at Trinity House and Armoury House, a visit to the Mermaid Theatre to see *The Inspector Calls*, and a visit to the Chinese Exhibition at Burlington House.[176] Robert Horton, celebrating his very distinguished naval ancestors, took the livery down river to Greenwich in the following year.[177]

As well as livery functions the Company has also taken part in City festivals. The Royal River Pageant held in 1953 was well supported by the Company who voted a substantial sum towards the cost and were represented by the Master, F. W. Gutridge I.S.O., the Wardens H. A. Gill, L. Bingham, A. W. Dentith, E. W. Watts F.C.A., C.C., the past Master F. Gillet, the Clerk and the Beadle.[178] In the event the pageant cost the Company much less than had been agreed and the Court accordingly sent a donation to the pageant committee which was in debt.[179] In 1962 the Company subscribed to the City Arts Trust Ltd., which runs the Festival of the City of London.[180] The festival is now a biannual event and a great tourist attraction.

In the last few years there has been a change of emphasis in the Company's thinking. No one could accuse the Court of having neglected its duties to the livery, indeed far otherwise, but there has been a new and more serious note. This has shown itself in a greater pre-occupation with wider charitable duties and in a determination to encourage and keep in contact with the trade.

The charitable fund set up in 1940 was, as we have seen, limited in its scope. The trust deed allowed for donations for the relief of freemen and their dependents or the employees of the trade, to appeals started by the Lord Mayor, to hospitals in the City and County of London and to other similar funds for the relief of poverty and suffering and distress. The Court of the late 'sixties thought this insufficient and, Counsel having recommended that a new trust fund should be made, one was set up in 1969.[181] An appeal had been made to the livery as early as 1966 and the new grants and donations were put in the new fund.[182] The liverymen responded very generously and the new fund is already able to do more than the old. Both funds are administered by a committee consisting of the Master and Wardens, the immediate Past Master and the Clerk.[183] In 1974 at the instigation of Robert Horton, Douglas Dunstan and Clifford Jeapes, Masters in 1974, 1973 and 1972 respectively,[184] the Court adopted London Homes for the Elderly as its most important charitable commitment. There was a most gratifying response to the decision and a number of liverymen volunteered to join a liaison committee with London Homes for the Elderly. They also gave money, although no appeal was made.[185] This charity could hardly have been bettered, its only limitations are to London and the old. It carries out one of the most venerable traditional duties of the livery companies; the housing of the old. It supplies one of the Welfare State's most heartbreaking inadequacies. In addition, the charity was a peculiarly pleasant choice for the Company because it was founded by Sir George Wilkinson Bt., K.C.V.O. Sir George was one of the best loved and most distinguished members of the Court. He was Master in 1943[186] and Lord Mayor in 1940.[187] He died in 1967.[188]

Although the Gold and Silver Wyre-Drawers have a Guild church of their own, St. James, Garlickhythe[189] where for 40 years The Company has held its Installation Service, they have always been concerned with the upkeep of other City churches, especially St. Mary Le Bow.[190] The appeal for St. Paul's was very near their hearts, and an appeal personally launched by the Master, Clifford Jeapes, in 1972 received a gratifying response.[191] The livery have attended the United Guilds Service there in March every year since 1944.[192]

The Company has widened its activities in a most unusual direction. In 1969 on the inspiration of Past Master Leslie Boyd the Company adopted an appropriately small ship, a submarine called H.M.S. Olympus. Lt. Commander Richard Channon and Lt. St. John Steiner came to the Court dinner in January 1970 and presented the Company with a plaque of the submarine's Coat of Arms. The Company had already given the lower deck beer and the officers a Thuya wood cigarette box for the ward room at Christmas.[193] The idea is that the Company should be able to help any member of the crew in any financial difficulties which are beyond the scope of the Service charitable organisations. In 1972 past Master Andrew Johnson was appointed Ship's Agent and attended the recommissioning ceremony after the submarine was refitted in that year.[194] During 1972 and 1973 she was on duty in Northern waters[195] but in 1974 the Master, mindful of his naval forbears, went to sea in her.[196] In 1975 she put into London and many of the livery and their families were able to visit her,[197] and were received most hospitably by the ship's company.

Probably more important than any other post war development has been the Court's increased interest in the trade, particularly in trade education. The Company has more than continued its tradition of interesting and valuable exhibitions. In 1961 Dennis Johnson organised a trade exhibit for the Commonwealth Training Week Exhibition, which was very well received. The Court contributed some money towards this, as also to the expense of the Gold Lace and Embroiderers' Association, who were also exhibiting. The livery with true devotion saved the cost of a caretaker by providing a rota of guardians.[198] During his year as Master, Robert Horton, then the chairman of Stephen Simpson, organised an exhibition for the livery at Goldsmiths' Hall which was breathtakingly lovely and could well have attracted the public. The displays included H.A.C. 18th century Grenadier caps, replicas of coronation gloves lent by the Glovers' Company, working demonstrations of embroidery and the making of embroidery materials. There was also a film made by Mr. Walmsley, also of Stephen Simpson, which readers of this book after so many tedious descriptions might well long to see. It showed how gold and silver wire is made and how gold wire and thread laces are produced.[199]

Since the war the Company has subscribed regularly to the City and Guilds of London Institute which runs the City and Guilds examinations.[200] In July 1958 L. Murray Johnson was appointed to represent the Company on the Council of the Institute.[201] In 1955 Herbert Toye suggested that this interest in education should be increased by awarding two prizes yearly to encourage fine workmanship and processing in the Company's craft. One prize was to be given for hand embroidery with gold and silver wire, the other for design and workmanship. The first judges were C. D. Stillwell and Roland Benton.[202] In 1971 the Master Frank O. M. Smith started a new scheme which invited students of the Royal College of Arts to compete in producing designs for gold and silver wire in new ways. The prize given by Mr. Smith was a hundred pounds. In the first year of the award 1972 it was so difficult to choose between the entries that Robert Horton gave a second prize from Stephen Simpson Ltd.[203] In 1973 two prizes of £100 were awarded.[204] and in 1974 one of £100 and two of £25 were dispensed.[205] The Company's contacts with the Royal College had started before this when the college first received its charter. The new provost had no official gown; such items are expensive, especially when embroidered with gold and silver wire. The Company accordingly gave the embroidery materials for the robe, and the Provost, Sir Colin Anderson, F.R.S.A. donned it for the admiration of the livery at the banquet in 1967.[206]

Besides contacts with the Royal College of Art, the Company has established connections with the Royal School of Needlework. In 1961 the School ran into financial difficulties and was threatened with being closed down. H.R.H. Princess Alice, Countess of Athlone, an Honorary Freeman, of the Gold and Silver Wyre-Drawers Company, asked the City Livery Companies to help, and those connected with cloth or needlework did so. A committee consisting of the representatives of the eight companies concerned was formed. These were the Broderers', the Clothworkers', the Needlemakers', the Weavers', the Mercers', the Drapers', the Merchant Taylors', and the Gold and Silver Wyre-Drawers'. The Royal School was saved, and in gratitude and expectancy the Dowager Countess of Bessborough asked for two representatives from the livery companies to sit on the executive committee of the School. The Livery Companies' committee agreed that one of these representatives should be supplied by the Gold and Silver Wyre-Drawer's.[207] The obvious person was Herbert Toye and he was the Company's permanent representative until he died in 1968.[208] The company maintains two apprentices at the school and on several occasions they have been invited to the annual Banquet.

For an ancient institution, with a constitution that is unchanged since it was laid down in 1693, and functions which preoccupy the modern court that are only a development of those agreed in its first byelaws, the Company seems remarkably modern. It still cares for those in need, watches and encourages the trade and is proud to take that part in the pageantry and government of the city to which it first attained in 1780, but the great 20th-century cries of racialism and anti-feminism have left it unscathed. The Gold and Silver Wyre-Drawers have always been open-minded and remain so, they accepted women from the beginning and still do so.[209] There is no reason to suppose that in the 21st century they will not be the same, quite as modern as anybody ever is. They have always been men of enterprise and good sense, moving with the times, but not discarding those customs of the past which are honourable and useful. Theirs has been an example of goodwill which has been admirably exemplified by the motto of their Coat of Arms. 'Amicitiam trahit Amor'; Love draws forth friendship.

Notes

The following abbreviations have been used

B.M.   British Museum
C.P.M.R.   Calendar of Plea and Memoranda Rolls
C.S.P.   Calendar of State Papers
C.S.P.D.   Calendar of State Papers Domestic
H.C.J.   House of Commons Journals
H.L.J.   House of Lords Journals

Chapter I

1. Doreen Yarwood, *English Costume from the Second Century B.C. to 1967* (1969), p. 4
2. *Ibid.*, p. 8
3. Horace Stewart, *History of the Worshipful Company of Gold and Silver Wyre-Drawers* (1891), p. 6
4. *Ibid.*, p. 6. *Exodus*, XXXIX, 2, 3
5. *Ibid.*, p. 8
6. Lucius Apuleius, *The Golden Ass*, translated Robert Graves. (1960), p. 270
7. Vulgar French Song, 'Saint Eloy n'est pas mort parcequ'il bond encore'
8. Donald Attwater, *The Penguin Dictionary of Saints*, p. 112
9. Horace Stewart, *History of the Worshipful Company of Gold and Silver Wyre-Drawers* (1891), p. 7
10. *Ibid.*, pp. 13, 14
11. *Ibid.*, and Violet Pamphlets. B.M.714, h.12
12. Information given by David Lloyd Esq., Director of the Royal School of Needlework
13. Horace Stewart, *History of the Worshipful Company of Gold and Silver Wyre-Drawers* (1891), p. 14
14. George Cameron Stone and Jack Brussel, *A Glossary of the Construction Decoration and Use of Arms a,d Armor in all countries and in all times* (1961), p. 306
15. Philip E. Jones, ed., *Calendar of Plea and Memoranda Rolls*, 1458–1482, p. 112
16. Horace Stewart, *History of the Worshipful Company of Gold and Silver Wyre-Drawers* (1891), p. 29; H.C.J., Vol. I
17. *Ibid.*, p. 14
18. *Ibid.*, p. 17
19. Stephen Simpson, T.D., D.L., M.A., *History of the Firm of Stephen Simpson 1829–1929* (1929), p. 25
20. C.S.P.D., p. 330, 13 September 1655
21. See ChapterIII
22. *The Book of Trades or Library of the Useful Arts*, part III. (1805), p. 57; C.S.P.D., p. 330, 1655 September 13

23 Stephen Simpson, T.D., D.L., M.A., *History of the Firm of Stephen Simpson 1829–1929* (1929), pp. 15 and 16
24 *The Book of Trades or Library of Useful Arts, Part III.* (1805), pp. 57–59
25 Proposals to his Highness, Oliver Lord Protector of England etc. Humble proposal of many hundred spinners. Thomas Violet 1651–1662; B.M.714 h.12, p. 145
26 Information given by J. F. Walmsley Esq., Managing Director of Stephen Simpson (Northern Counties) Ltd.
27 Information given by E. C. Fitch Esq., late managing director, John Sharp (Gold Thread) Ltd.
28 For Regulating the Manufacture of Gold and Silver Thread 1651. Thomas Violet; B.M.714 h.12, pp. 98–123

Chapter II

1 Horace Stewart, *History of the Worshipful Company of Gold and Silver Wyre-Drawers* (1891), p. 11; *Encyclopaedia Britannica*
2 *Ibid.*, p. 12; *Riley's Memorials of London Life*
3 *Ibid.*, p. 12. *Archaeologia*, Vol. III
4 Phillis Cunnington and Catherine Lucas, *Costume of Births, Marriages and Deaths* (1972), pp. 164–166; *Church Historians* (Trans: J. Stevenson), Vol. I, pp. 781–5
5 Bede, *A History of the English Church and People.* (Translated by Leo Sherley Price), (1956), pp. 260–261
6 Patricia Wardle, *Guide to English Embroidery* (1970), pp. 6–8
7 Horace Stewart, *History of the Worshipful Company of Gold and Silver Wyre-Drawers* (1891), p. 12; *C.S.P.* Rolls of Parliament, Vol. II, p. 47
8 *Ibid.*, p. 19; *Historical Books*, Vol. II
9 John Burnett, *A History of the Cost of Living* (1969), p. 34
10 Horace Stewart, *History of the Worshipful Company of Gold and Silver Wyre-Drawers* (1891), p. 14; *C.S.P.* Rolls of Parliament, 2 Henry VI, Cap. X, Vol. IV, p. 255, p. 18 and Henry VII, Cap. 22
11 *Ibid.*, p. 20; *C.S.P.* Harleian No. 1419. Planché
12 *Ibid.*, p. 20; *C.S.P.*
13 *Ibid.*, p. 21; *C.S.P.*
14 *Ibid.*, p. 21; *Archaeologia*, Vol. XII
15 Patricia Wardle, *Guide to English Embroidery* (1970), p. 10
16 Marjorie B. Honeybourne, M.A., F.S.A., ed., *London Topographical Record* Vol. XXIII (1974); A. C. Edwards, *Sir John Petre and some Elizabethan Tradesmen*, pp. 80–81
17 Horace Stewart, *History of the Worshipful Company of Gold and Silver Wyre-Drawers* (1891), p. 19; *C.S.P.* Rolls of Parliament, Henry VIII, Cap. 6
18 Marjorie B. Honeybourne, M.A., F.S.A., ed., *London Topographical Record* Vol. XXIII. (1974); A. C. Edwards, *Sir John Petre and some Elizabethan Tradesmen*, p. 80
19 Philip E. Jones, ed., *Calendar of Plea and Memoranda Rolls*, Vol. 1458–1482 (1961) pp. 112, 113
20 Horace Stewart, *History of the Worshipful Company of Gold and Silver Wyre-Drawers* (1891), p. 20; *Historical Books*, Vol. II
21 *Ibid.*, p. 29; *H.C.J.*, Vol. I
22 Marjorie B. Honeybourne, M.A., F.S.A., ed., *London Topographical Record*, Vol. XXIII (1974); A. C. Edwards, *Sir John Petre and some Elizabethan Tradesmen*, pp. 86, 87
23 Horace Stewart, *History of the Worshipful Company of Gold and Silver Wyre-Drawers* (1891); *Archaeologia*, Vol. 41

24 Proposals to his Highness, Oliver Lord Protector of England, etc. Humble Proposal of many Hundred Spinners. Thomas Violet 1651–1662; B.M.714, h.12
25 Proposals to his Highness, Oliver Lord Protector of England, etc. Thomas Violet 1651–1662; B.M.714, h.12; Horace Stewart, *History of the Worshipful Company of Gold and Silver Wyre-Drawers* (1891); p. 14; *C.S.P.* Rolls of Parliament, 2 Henry VI Cap. X, Vol. IV, pp. 27, 255; Analytical Index to the Remembrancia
26 The case of the Manufacturers of Gilt and Silver Wire. Post 1713; B.M.1887, p. 60
27 For Regulating the Manufacture of Gold and Silver Thread 1651. Thomas Violet. B.M.714, h.12, pp. 98–123
28 Proposals to his Highness, Oliver Lord Protector of England, etc. Humble Proposal of many Hundred Spinners. Thomas Violet. B.M.714, h.12, p. 102
29 The case of the Manufacturers of Gilt and Silver Wire. Post 1713; B.M.1887, p. 60
30 John Burnett, *A History of the Cost of Living* (1969), p. 131
31 Proposals to his Highness, Oliver Lord Protector of England, etc. Humble Proposals of many Hundred Spinners. Thomas Violet, 1651–1662; B.M.714, h.12, p. 145
32 To the King's Most Excellent Majesty and the Lords Spiritual and Temporal and Commons in Parliament. Thomas Violet: Petition for the renewal of his patent. B.M., b.b. 20, 1479
33 For Regulating the Manufacture of Gold and Silver Thread, 1651. Thomas Violet, B.M.714, h.12
34 Horace Stewart, *History of the Worshipful Company of Gold and Silver Wyre-Drawers* (1891), p. 14; *C.S.P.* Roll of Parliament, 2 Henry VI, Cap. X, Vol. IV, p. 255
35 *C.S.P.D.*, p. 330, 13 September 1655
36 For Regulating the Manufacture of Gold and Silver Thread. Thomas Violet, 1651. B.M.714, h.12, pp. 98–123
37 The Perfect Weekly Account, 27 December 1648–31 January 1649
38 Horace Stewart, *History of the Worshipful Company of Gold and Silver Wyre-Drawers*, p. 20; Harleian No. 1419, Planché
39 Marjorie B. Honeybourne, M.A., F.S.A., ed., *London Topographical Record*, Vol. XXIII (1974); A. C. Edwards, *Sir John Petre and some Elizabethan Tradesmen*, p. 83
40 Girdlers Company Records, Book of Benefactors, 15 August 1575
41 Vintners Company Records, AO/1, p. 50
42 Horace Stewart, *History of the Worshipful Company of Gold and Silver Wyre-Drawers* (1891), p. 22
43 Ibid.; Historical Books, Vol. II
44 Marjorie B. Honeybourne, M.A., F.S.A., ed., *London Topographical Record*, Vol. (1974); A. C. Edwards, *Sir John Petre and some Elizabethan Tradesmen*, p. 80
45 Ibid., p. 83
46 Ibid., p. 84
47 Ibid., p. 82
48 John Burnett, *A History of the Cost of Living*. (1969), p. 90
49 Ibid., p. 125
50 Ibid., p. 89
51 Ibid., p. 125
52 S. T. Bindoff, *Tudor England* (1950), p. 119
53 R. H. Tawney, *Business and Politics under James I: Lionel Cranfield, Merchant and Minister* (1958), p. 138
54 S. T. Bindoff, *Tudor England* (1950), p. 122
55 John Burnett, *A History of the Cost of Living*. (1969), p. 88
56 Horace Stewart, *History of the Worshipful Company of Gold and Silver Wyre-Drawers* (1891), p. 28; H.C.J., Vol. I, p. 511; Cobbett's Parliamentary History, Vol. I, p. 1198

57 Samuel Rawson Gardiner, *Constitutional Documents of the Puritan Revolution, 1625–1660* (1958); The Grand Remonstrance Article 37, p. 212
58 *C.S.P.D.*, 1624, Vol. CLXII, p. 207
59 *C.S.P.D.*, 1624, Vol. CLXII, p. 207; *C.S.P.D.*, 1624, Vol. CLXIX, p. 300
60 For Regulating the Manufacture of Gold and Silver Thread. Thomas Violet, 1651. B.M.714, h.12, pp.98–123
61 Horace Stewart, *History of the Worshipful Company of Gold and Silver Wyre-Drawers* (1891). pp. 24, 25, 4 February 1617/18: Quoted in *Mint Records Books*, I, p. 45
62 *Ibid.*, p. 28; *H.C.J.*, Vol. I, p. 511
63 For Regulating the Manufacture of Gold and Silver Thread. Thomas Violet, 1651. B.M.714, h.12, pp. 98–123
64 The Great Trappaner of England discovered. B.M.714, h.12
65 For Regulating the Manufacture of Gold and Silver Thread. Thomas Violet, 1651. B.M.714, h.12, pp. 98–123
66 *Ibid.*
67 *Ibid.*
68 *Ibid.*
69 Proposals to his Highness, Lord Protector Cromwell. Thomas Violet, B.M.714, h.12, p. 147
70 For Regulating the Manufacture of Gold and Silver Thread. Thomas Violet, 1651. B.M.714, h.12, pp. 98–123
71 *Ibid.*
72 Proposals to his Highness, Oliver Lord Protector of England. Thomas Violet, B.M.714, h.12, p. 124
73 *Ibid., passim.*
74 To the King's Excellent Majesty and the Lords Spiritual and Temporal and Commons in Parliament, B.M. b.b., 20, 1479
Advertisement for the Working Cutlers within the City of London and suburbs thereof
75 A petition against the Jews. Thomas Violet, B.M.714, h.12
76 Phillis Cunnington and Catherine Lucas, *Costume of Births, Marriages and Deaths* (1972), p. 159, 18 & 19 Car. II, Cap. 4
77 *Ibid.*, p. 140; *The Gentlemen's Magazine*, Vol. 17, pp. 264, 265
78 John Burnett, *A History of the Cost of Living* (1969), p. 90
79 Sonnet LXXX
80 *Epithalamion*
81 *At a Solemn Musick*

Chapter III

1 Guildhall Manuscripts 2448
2 Horace Stewart, *History of the Company of Gold and Silver Wyre-Drawers* (1891), p. 57; *Repertories* Vol. 95, fol. 229
3 *Ibid., Rep.*, Vol. 95, fol. 246
4 *Ibid.*
5 *Ibid., Rep.*, Vol. 97, fol. 433
6 Guildhall Manuscripts 2448
7 Guildhall Manuscripts 2450
8 Horace Stewart, *History of the Company of Gold and Silver Wyre-Drawers* (1891), p. 50; Goldsmiths' Documents, 6 June 1664

9 *Ibid.*, pp. 53, 54, 55. Goldsmiths' Documents, 23 September 1664
10 *Ibid.*, p. 61
11 Guildhall Manuscripts 2452/1
12 *London Past and Present* (1891), Vol. 2, p. 115
13 Horace Stewart, *History of the Company of Gold and Silver Wyre-Drawers* (1891), p. 49; C.S.P.D.
14 *Ibid.*, C.S.P.D.
15 *Ibid.*, p. 52; Goldsmiths' Company Manuscripts 1 June 1664
16 *Ibid.*, p. 50; C.S.P.D.
17 Guildhall Manuscripts 2448
18 Guildhall Manuscripts 2451/1, p. 126
19 Guildhall Manuscripts 2451/2, 8 August 1723
20 Guildhall Manuscripts 2451/3, 11 January 1770
21 Guildhall Manuscripts 2451/3, 12 November 1767
22 Guildhall Manuscripts 2448
23 Guildhall Manuscripts 2451/3, 13 December 1770
24 *Ibid.*, 2451/1, p. 3
25 *Ibid.*, p. 21
26 *Ibid.*, p. 23
27 *Ibid.*, p. 56
28 *Ibid.*, p. 132
29 *Ibid.*, pp. 10, 15, 17, 22
30 *Ibid.*, p. 168
31 *Ibid.*, pp. 17, 32 and elsewhere
32 *Ibid.*, pp. 27, 32 and elsewhere
33 *Ibid.*, p. 25 and elsewhere
34 *Ibid.*, p. 84
35 *Ibid.*, p. 128
36 *Ibid.*, p. 130
37 *Ibid.*, p. 119
38 *Ibid.*, p. 125
39 *Ibid.*, p. 125
40 *Ibid.*, p. 83
41 *Ibid.*, p. 126
42 *Ibid.*, p. 61
43 *Ibid.*, p. 20
44 *Ibid.*, p. 121
45 *Ibid.*, p. 61
46 *Ibid.*, p. 130
47 *Ibid.*, pp. 116/7
48 *Ibid.*, pp. 116/7
49 Guildhall Manuscripts 2448
50 Guildhall Manuscripts 2451/1, p. 147
51 *Ibid.*, p. 92
52 *Ibid.*, p. 89
53 *Ibid.*, p. 127
54 *Ibid.*, p. 17
55 *Ibid.*, 3 December 1701, p. 149
56 *Ibid.*, 2448

57 *Ibid.*
58 *Ibid.*, 2451/1, p. 133
59 *Ibid.*, pp. 62, 63, 64, 65, 69
60 *Ibid.*, p. 71
61 *Ibid.*
62 Horace Stewart, *History of the Company of Gold and Silver Wyre-Drawers* (1891), Appendix
63 Guildhall Manuscripts 2451/1, p. 75
64 Horace Stewart, *History of the Company of Gold and Silver Wyre-Drawers* (1891), Appendix
65 Guildhall Manuscripts 2451/1, p. 88
66 Guildhall Manuscripts 2451/1
67 *Ibid.*, pp. 10, 39 and 40
68 *Ibid.*, 2451/2, 17 December 1719
69 *Ibid.*, 2451/1
70 *Ibid.*, 2451/2, 17 December 1719
71 *Ibid.*, 2451/1
72 *Ibid.*, p. 38
73 *Ibid.*, p. 56
74 *Ibid.*, p. 41
75 *Ibid.*, p. 90
76 Guildhall Manuscripts 2451/1
77 Guildhall Manuscripts 2451/1, p. 110
78 *Ibid.*, p. 186
79 *Ibid.*, pp. 136, 138
80 Guildhall Manuscripts 2448
81 Guildhall Manuscripts Quarterage books
82 Guildhall Manuscripts 2448
83 Guildhall Manuscripts 2452/1
84 Guildhall Manuscripts 2452/1; 1700
85 Guildhall Manuscripts 2451/1, p. 89
86 *Ibid.*, p. 124
87 *Ibid.*, p. 184
88 *Ibid.*, February 1703/4
89 Some notes on the History of the Vintners Company, September 1969
90 Guildhall Manuscripts 2451/1, p. 191
91 Horace Stewart, *History of the Worshipful Company of Gold and Silver Wyre-Drawers* (1891), p. 55; H.C.J., Vol. XI, p. 364

Chapter IV
1 J. H. Plumb, *England in the Eighteenth Century* (1974), p. 24
2 Guildhall Manuscripts 2451/3, 12 November 1767
3 *Ibid.*, 14 May 1767, 12 November 1767, 10 December 1767
4 *Ibid.*, 8 September 1768
5 *Ibid.*, 14 May 1767
6 *Ibid.*, 13 December 1770
7 *Ibid.*, 9 May 1754
8 *Ibid.*, 13 April 1769
9 *Ibid.*, 10 May 1764

10   D'Arblay IV, 243–250
11   Doreen Yarwood, *English Costume from the Second Century B.C. to 1967* (1969), Plate VIII, Portrait of the Countess of Mar 1715, in the possession of the Earl of Mar and Kellie, K.T.
12   Guildhall Manuscripts 2541/3, 12 June 1766
13   A. S. Turbeville, *English Men and Manners in the Eighteenth Century* (1957), p. 95
14   John Burnett, *A History of the Cost of Living* (1969)
15   Guildhall Manuscripts 2451/3, 14 January 1747/8
16   *Ibid.*, 14 January 1768
17   *Ibid.*, 10 September 1761
18   *Ibid.*, 8 September 1768, 13 November 1766
19   *Ibid.*, 8 November 1764
20   *Ibid.*, 10 January 1765
21   *Ibid.*, 13 November 1766
22   *Ibid.*, 14 January 1768
23   *Ibid.*, 8 September 1768
24   Guildhall Manuscripts 2452/2, 10 July 1755
25   The Case of the Manufacturers of Gilt and Silver Wire Post 1713, B.M.1887
26   An appeal to the Nobility and Gentry. Printed for R. Griffiths at the Dunciad 1755
27   Guildhall Manuscripts 2451/2, 23 June 1720, 28 June 1720
28   Horace Stewart, *History of the Worshipful Company of Gold and Silver Wyre-Drawers* (1891), p. 83; H.L.J., XXVI, p. 144
     Ibid., p. 84 and Photostat Copy of the Act kindly lent to me by D. H. L. Johnson, Esq.
29   Horace Stewart, *History of the Worshipful Company of Gold and Silver Wyre-Drawers* (1891), p. 84; H.C.J., XXIV, pp. 379, 388
30   Guildhall Manuscripts 2451/2
31   Horace Stewart, *History of the Worshipful Company of Gold and Silver Wyre-Drawers* (1891), p. 85; H.C.J., XXIV
32   *Ibid., H.C.J.*, XXIV, pp. 397, 398
33   *Ibid., H.C.J.*, XXIV, p. 399
34   *Ibid., H.C.J.*, XXIV, p. 404
35   *Ibid., H.C.J.*, XXIV, p. 412
36   *Ibid.*, pp. 74, 75; *H.C.J.*, XXIV, pp. 397, 398
37   Guildhall Manuscripts 2451/2, 14 April 1720
38   Guildhall Manuscripts 2451/3, 8 January 1761
39   Guildhall Manuscripts 2451/2, 8 January 1729
40   Guildhall Manuscripts 2451/3, 10 April 1760
41   *Ibid.*, 10 July 1766
42   *Ibid.*, 8 May 1766
43   *Ibid.*, 9 February 1769
44   *Ibid.*, 13 April 1769
45   *Ibid.*, 13 June 1771
46   *Ibid.*, 8 August 1771
47   Guildhall Manuscripts 2449 Byelaw, 12 November 1761
48   *Ibid.*
49   *Ibid.*
50   Guildhall Manuscripts 2451/4, 3 March 1790
51   J. H. Plumb, *England in the Eighteenth Century* (1974), pp. 118, 119
52   *Ibid.*, pp. 119–123

53 *Ibid.*, p. 123
54 Guildhall Manuscripts 2451/4, 19 October 1789
55 Elizabeth Gaskell, *North and South*
56 Guildhall Manuscripts 2451/4, 26 October 1789
57 *Ibid.*, 9 November 1789
58 *Ibid.*, 13 January 1791
59 *Ibid.*, 10 December 1789
60 *Ibid.*, 13 January 1791, 31 March 1791
61 *Ibid.*, 3 March 1790
62 *Ibid.*, 3 March 1790, 8 April 1790
63 Guildhall Manuscripts 2451/1, 337
64 Guildhall Manuscripts 2451/2, 22 October 1735
65 Guildhall Manuscripts 2451/3, 12 January 1758
66 Guildhall Manuscripts 2451/2, 12 November 1724
67 *Ibid.*, 2451/1, 1716
68 Guildhall Manuscripts 2451/2, 1741
69 *See* Chapter VII
70 Guildhall Manuscripts 2451/2, 1743
71 Letter from 'Windsor Herald', 9 July 1975
72 Horace Stewart, *History of the Worshipful Company of Gold and Silver Wyre-Drawers* (1891), p. 4
73 Guildhall Manuscripts 2451/2, 17 December 1719
74 Horace Stewart, *History of the Worshipful Company of Gold and Silver Wyre-Drawers* (1891), p. 89
75 Guildhall Manuscripts 2451/4, 10 November 1788
76 Letter from 'Windsor Herald', 9 July 1975
77 Guildhall Manuscripts 2448
78 *Ibid.*, and 2451/2, 17 December 1719
79 Guildhall Manuscripts 2451/4, 11 January 1781
80 Guildhall Manuscripts 2448
81 Guildhall Manuscripts 2451/3, 11 December 1755
82 Guildhall Manuscripts 2451/3, 12 February 1761
83 Guildhall Manuscripts 2451/2, 1731
84 Guildhall Manuscripts 2451/4, 4 November 1799
85 Horace Stewart, *History of the Worshipful Company of Gold and Silver Wyre-Drawers* (1891), p. 69
86 Guildhall Manuscripts 2451/3, 11 December 1766
87 Horace Stewart, *History of the Worshipful Company of Gold and Silver Wyre-Drawers* (1891), p. 98 and Guildhall Manuscripts 2451/2, 2451/3, 2451/4 passim
88 Guildhall Manuscripts 2451/4, 14 January 1802, 11 March 1802
89 *Ibid.*, 10 March 1808
90 *Ibid.*, 2448
91 *Ibid.*, 2451/2, 1 March 1719/20, 10 March 1719/20, 9 April 1720
92 *Ibid.*, 2449, 18 July 1780
93 *Ibid.*, 2451/4, 13 January 1780, 10 August 1780
94 *Ibid.*, 9 November 1780
95 *Ibid.*, 2448
96 *Ibid.*, 2451/4, 3 March 1790
97 *Ibid.*
98 *Ibid.*, 2449
99 *Ibid.*, 2451/4, 8 January 1784

Chapter V
1. A. Goodwin, *The French Revolution* (1959), pp. 75–7
2. A. S. Turbeville, *English Men and Manners in the eighteenth century* (1957), p. 96
3. Phillis Cunnington and Catherine Lucas, *Costume for Births, Marriages and Deaths* (1972), p. 100
4. *Ibid.*, p. 103
5. *Ibid.*, pp. 100, 101
6. *Ibid.*, p. 109
7. *Ibid.*, p. 103
8. *Ibid.*, pp. 110, 111
9. Piers Compton, *Cardigan of Balaclava* (1972), p. 64
10. Arthur Bryant, *The Age of Elegance, 1812–1822* (1958), pp. 174, 299
11. Cash Book of Barrett & Corney 1785–1802, 19 April 1788
12. Guildhall Manuscripts 2451/4, 7 January 1831
13. Horace Stewart, *History of the Worshipful Company of Gold and Silver Wyre-Drawers* (1891), p. 101
14. Guildhall Manuscripts 2451/4, 16 October 1810
15. *The Firm of Stephen Simpson, 1829–1929* (1929), p. 25 and from information given by E. C. Finch Esq. and F. H. Leigh Esq.
16. *The Firm of Stephen Simpson, 1829–1929* (1929), pp. 32 and 34
17. Guildhall Manuscripts 2451/4 *passim.*, 1800–1820
18. *Ibid.*, 9 November 1796
19. *Ibid.*, 12 January 1804
20. *Ibid.*, 16 March 1820, 6 July 1820
21. *Ibid.*, 11 January 1821
22. *Ibid.*, 17 January 1822
23. *Ibid.*, 1796
24. *Ibid.*, 1809
25. *Ibid.*, 9 January 1800, 9 October 1800
26. *Ibid.*, 16 October 1810
27. *Ibid.*, 1824
28. *Ibid.*, 21 June 1827
29. *Ibid.*, 25 January 1838
30. *Ibid.*, 12 January 1826
31. *Ibid.*
32. *Ibid.*, 27 April 1826
33. *Ibid.*
34. *Ibid.*
35. *Ibid.*, 8 January 1829
36. *Ibid.*, 10 January 1828
37. *Ibid.*, 12 January 1832
38. *Ibid.*, 7 January 1831
39. Horace Stewart, *History of the Worshipful Company of Gold and Silver Wyre-Drawers* (1891), p. 99
40. Guildhall Manuscripts 2451/4, 9 November 1831
41. *Ibid.*, 11 January 1843
42. *Ibid.*, 12 January 1832
43. *Ibid.*
44. *Ibid.*, 10 January 1833

45 *Ibid.*, 9 January 1834
46 Horace Stewart, *History of the Worshipful Company of Gold and Silver Wyre-Drawers* (1891), p. 102
47 Guildhall Manuscripts 2451/4, 25 January 1838
48 Horace Stewart, *History of the Worshipful Company of Gold and Silver Wyre-Drawers* (1891), pp. 102–103
49 *Ibid.*, p. 103
50 Cash Book, 1884–1924, 1887
51 Horace Stewart, *History of the Worshipful Company of Gold and Silver Wyre-Drawers* (1891), p. 103
52 *Ibid.*, p. 103
53 *Ibid.*, p. 104
54 *Ibid.*, p. 105
55 *Ibid.*, p. 104
56 Salters Company's Documents, 1883/4
57 Horace Stewart, *History of the Worshipful Company of the Gold and Silver Wyre-Drawers* (1891), p. 104
58 *Ibid.*, p. 105
59 *Ibid.*, p. 106
60 *Ibid.*, pp. 120–121
61 The Firm of Stephen Simpson, 1829–1929 (1929), p. 32
62 Horace Stewart, *History of the Worshipful Company of Gold and Silver Wyre-Drawers* (1891), p. 106
63 Cash Book, 1884–1924, 1889
64 Horace Stewart, *History of the Worshipful Company of Gold and Silver Wyre-Drawers* (1891), pp. 106–7
65 Cash Book, 1884–1924, 1891–2
66 *Ibid.*, 1884–1924, 1886, 1888, 1889
67 *Ibid.*, 1888, 1890–91
68 Horace Stewart, *History of the Worshipful Company of Gold and Silver Wyre-Drawers* (1891), p. 104
69 Cash Book, 1884–1924, 1891–2
70 Horace Stewart, *History of the Worshipful Company of Gold and Silver Wyre-Drawers* (1891), p. 104
71 *Ibid.*, 100, 109
72 *Ibid.*, 109
73 *Ibid.*, pp. 104, 105
74 Report of the City Livery Commission
75 Guildhall Manuscripts 2451/4, 9 January 1834
76 Report of the City Livery Commission
77 Cash Book, 1884–1894, 1893–94
78 Report of the City Livery Commission
79 Horace Stewart, *History of the Worshipful Company of Gold and Silver Wyre-Drawers* (1891), p. 106
80 *Ibid.*, p. 104; Cash Book, 1884–1924
81 Cash Book, 1884–1924, 1898
82 Inventory of the Company's plate made by Asprey and Birch and Gaydon Ltd.
83 Horace Stewart, *History of the Worshipful Company of Gold and Silver Wyre-Drawers* (1891), p. 104
84 Inventory of the Company's plate made by Asprey and Birch and Gaydon Ltd.
85 *Ibid.*
86 Guildhall Manuscripts 2452/2, 10 July 1755
87 Cash Book, 1884–1924, 1888

Chapter VI

1. History of the Firm of Stephen Simpson, 1829–1929 (1929), p. 16
2. *Ibid.*, p. 51
3. *Ibid.*, p. 52
4. *Ibid.*, p. 16
5. *Ibid.*, p. 19
6. *Ibid.*, p. 19
7. Horace Stewart, *History of the Worshipful Company of Gold and Silver Wyre-Drawers* (1891), p. 106
8. Information supplied by Dennis Johnson, Esq.
9. History of the Firm of Stephen Simpson, 1829–1929 (1929), p. 17
10. Cash Book of Barrett and Corney, 1785–1802, October 1789–September 1790
11. *Ibid.*, 26 November 1799
12. *Ibid.*, 7 and 12 October 1789
13. *Ibid.*, 23 April 1790
14. *Ibid.*, 9 May 1789
15. *Ibid.*, 21 January 1789
16. *Ibid.*, 23 April 1790
17. *Ibid.*, 27 February 1787
18. *Ibid.*, 4 August 1787
19. *Ibid.*, 1 February 1790
20. *Ibid.*, 21 May 1790
21. *Ibid.*, 3 October 1786
22. *Ibid.*, 22 July 1787
23. *Ibid.*, 4 September 1786 *et passim*
24. *Ibid.*, 11 August 1789
25. *Ibid.*, 21 April 1794
26. *Ibid.*, 1 August 1786, 6 July 1787, 20 March 1794 *et passim*
27. *Ibid.*, 6 July 1787
28. *Ibid.*, 22 July 1786
29. *Ibid.*, 31 July 1786
30. *Ibid.*, 15 May 1787
31. *Ibid.*, 21 January 1786
32. *Ibid.*, 24 January 1786
33. *Ibid.*, 27 January 1786
34. *Ibid.*, 24 January 1786
35. *Ibid.*, 13 February 1786
36. *Ibid.*
37. *Ibid.*, 29 March 1786
38. *Ibid.*, 22 April 1786
39. *Ibid.*, 2 June 1786
40. *Ibid.*, 13 July 1789
41. *Burke's Peerage, Baronetage and Knightage* (102nd. Edition), p. 1779
42. Cash Book of Barrett and Corney, 1785–1802: 17 January 1788
43. *Ibid.*, 21 April 1794
44. *Ibid.*, 20 March 1794
45. *Ibid.*, 6 June 1786
46. *Ibid.*, 12 August 1786
47. *Ibid.*, 16 August 1787

48 *Ibid.*, 26 November 1787
49 *Ibid.*, 4 January 1786
50 *Ibid.*, As 45–49 above and 16 March 1789
51 John Burnett, *A History of the Cost of Living* (1969), p. 180
52 Cash Book of Barrett and Corney, 1785–1802: 16 March 1789
53 *Ibid.*, 16 June 1786
54 *Ibid.*, 21 May 1789
55 *Ibid.*, 19 October 1787
56 *Ibid.*, 23 November 1787
57 *Ibid.*, 27 May 1788
58 *Ibid.*, 31 July 1788
59 *Ibid.*, 18 March 1788
60 *Ibid.*, 13 July 1789
61 *Ibid.*, 9 September 1789
62 *Ibid.*, 21 February 1789
63 *Ibid.*, 26 June 1789
64 *Ibid.*, 26 December 1786 *et passim*
65 *Ibid.*, 9 May 1786
66 *Ibid.*, 5 January 1787
67 *Ibid.*, 8 November 1785
68 *Ibid.*, 9 November 1785
69 *Ibid.*, 12 November 1785
70 *Ibid.*, 2 April 1787
71 *Ibid.*, 12 May 1786
72 *Ibid.*, 25 May 1786
73 *Ibid.*, 29 May 1786
74 *Ibid.*, 5 June 1786
75 *Ibid.*, 8 June 1786
76 *Ibid.*, 24 March 1787
77 *Ibid.*, 28 March 1787
78 *Ibid.*, 17 May 1787
79 *Ibid.*, 9 June 1787
80 *Ibid.*, 6 June 1787
81 *Ibid.*, 2 July 1787
82 *Ibid.*, 27 July 1787
83 *Ibid.*, 26 September 1787
84 *Ibid.*
85 *Ibid.*
86 *Ibid.*
87 *Ibid.*, 5 November 1787
88 Receipt Book of Barrett and Corney 1785–1795: 31 December 1785
89 *Ibid.*, at quarter days
90 *Ibid.*, 31 December 1785, 23 June 1786, 21 October 1786
91 31 December 1785
92 *Ibid.*
93 *Ibid.*
94 *Ibid.*, 16 January 1786, 10 April 1786
95 *Ibid.*, 21 October 1786

96 *Ibid.*, 21 July 1787
97 History of the Firm of Stephen Simpson, 1829–1929 (1929), p. 20
98 *Ibid.*, p. 19
99 *Ibid.*, p. 9
100 *Ibid.*, pp. 19 and 20
101 *Ibid.*, p. 39
102 *Ibid.*, p. 19
103 Letter from Roland Benton, Esq. to the author dated 25 February 1976
104 List of the Court and Livery 1969
105 Information supplied by Dennis Johnson, Esq.
106 List of the Court and Livery 1969
107 Horace Stewart, *History of the Worshipful Company of Gold and Silver Wyre-Drawers* (1891), p. 120
108 List of the Court and Livery 1969
109 Information supplied by Philip Cresswell, Esq. C.C. and Dennis Johnson, Esq.
110 History of the Firm of Stephen Simpson, 1829–1929 (1929), p. 55
111 Sales Book of Benton and Johnson 1886–1890
112 History of the Firm of Stephen Simpson, 1829–1929 (1929), pp. 25 and 51
113 *Ibid.*, pp. 51 and 52
114 *Ibid.*, p. 52
115 Information supplied by E. H. Leigh, Esq. owner of G. L. Tootell
116 Information supplied by E. C. Fitch, Esq., Managing Director of John Sharp (Gold Thread) Ltd.
117 Information supplied by E. H. Leigh, Esq. and E. C. Fitch, Esq.
118 History of the Firm of Stephen Simpson, 1829–1929 (1929), p. 16
119 Information supplied by J. F. Walmsley, Esq., Managing Director of Stephen Simpson (Northern Counties) Ltd.
120 History of the Firm of Stephen Simpson, 1829–1929 (1929), p. 17
121 Information supplied by E. H. Leigh, Esq. and E. C. Fitch, Esq.
122 *Ibid.*
123 Information supplied by E. H. Leigh, Esq.
124 Information supplied by E. C. Fitch, Esq.
125 History of the Firm of Stephen Simpson, 1829–1929 (1929), pp. 40–43
126 Information supplied by E. H. Leigh, Esq. and E. C. Fitch, Esq.
127 History of the Firm of Stephen Simpson, 1829–1929 (1929), p. 17
128 *Ibid.*, p. 19
129 *Ibid.*
130 *Ibid.*, pp. 40–43
131 Information supplied by Dennis Johnson, Esq.
132 Letters from Roland Benton, Esq. to Robert Horton the author, dated 11 February 1976, 25 February 1976, 10 March 1976
133 History of the Firm of Stephen Simpson, 1829–1929 (1929), p. 16
134 Information supplied by E. C. Fitch, Esq.
135 Information supplied by E. H. Leigh, Esq.
136 History of the Firm of Stephen Simpson, 1829–1929 (1929), p. 16
137 *Ibid.*, p. 25
138 *Ibid.*, pp. 53 and 54
139 *Ibid.*, p. 26
140 *Ibid.*, p. 56
141 *Ibid.*, p. 31

142 *Ibid.*, p. 49
143 *Ibid.*, p. 50
144 *Ibid.*, pp. 17, 25 and 26
145 Information supplied by E. H. Leigh, Esq.
146 History of the Firm of Stephen Simpson, 1829–1929 (1929), p. 17
147 Elizabeth Gaskell, *North and South* (1968), pp. 105, 154–155
148 History of the Firm of Stephen Simpson, 1829–1929 (1929), p. 30
149 Pamela Horn, *The Victorian Country Child* (1974), p. 101
150 C. Aspin, *Lancashire, the first industrial society* (1969), p. 69
151 Information supplied by J. F. Walmsley, Esq.
152 Information supplied by Miss May Blades, and Mr. W. Jackman
153 Pamela Horn, *The Victorian Country Child* (1974), p. 101
154 John Burnett, *A History of the Cost of Living* (1969), p. 252
155 History of the Firm of Stephen Simpson, 1829–1929 (1929), p. 50
156 Information supplied by J. F. Walmsley, Esq.
157 History of the Firm of Stephen Simpson, 1829–1929 (1929), p. 50
158 *Ibid.*, p. 51
159 *Ibid.*, p. 55
160 Information supplied by E. C. Fitch, Esq.
161 Information supplied by E. H. Leigh, Esq.
162 History of the Firm of Stephen Simpson, 1829–1929 (1929), pp. 29 and 31
163 Letter from Mrs. Melene Kentish-Barnes to the author, dated 22 February 1976
164 Letter from Roland Benton, Esq. to the author, dated 25 February 1976
165 *Ibid.*
166 History of the Firm of Stephen Simpson, 1829–1929 (1929), pp. 40–43
167 Letter from Roland Benton, Esq. to the author, dated 25 February 1976
168 Information supplied by E. C. Fitch, Esq.
169 Information supplied by E. H. Leigh, Esq.
170 Information supplied by E. H. Leigh, Esq. and E. C. Fitch, Esq.
171 Information supplied by Dennis Johnson, Esq. and letter from Robert Horton, Esq., formerly Chairman of Stephen Simpson (est. 1829) Ltd. to the author, dated 14 December 1975
172 Information supplied by Dennis Johnson, Esq.
173 Information supplied by E. H. Leigh, Esq.
174 Information supplied by E. C. Fitch, Esq.
175 Information supplied by E. H. Leigh, Esq.
176 Information supplied by E. H. Leigh, Esq. and E. C. Fitch, Esq.
177 Information supplied by J. F. Walmsley, Esq.
178 Information supplied by E. C. Fitch, Esq. and Dennis Johnson, Esq.
179 History of the Firm of Stephen Simpson, 1829–1929 (1929), p. 55
180 *Ibid.*, p. 25
181 *Ibid.*, pp. 25, 26
182 *Ibid.*, p. 54
183 Information supplied by E. H. Leigh, Esq.
184 Information supplied by E. C. Fitch, Esq.
185 Information supplied by E. H. Leigh, Esq.
186 Letter from Robert Horton, Esq. to the author, dated 14 December 1975 and information supplied by E. C. Fitch, Esq.
187 Information supplied by E. H. Leigh, Esq.

188 Information supplied by E. C. Fitch, Esq.
189 Information supplied by Dennis Johnson, Esq.
190 Information supplied by J. F. Walmsley, Esq.
191 History of the Firm of Stephen Simpson, 1829–1929 (1929), p. 46
192 Information supplied by Dennis Johnson, Esq.
193 Letter from Robert Horton, Esq. to the author, dated 14 December 1975; information also supplied by Dennis Johnson, Esq., E. C. Fitch, Esq., and J. F. Walmsley, Esq.
194 Information supplied by E. H. Leigh, Esq.
195 *Ibid.* and information supplied by J. F. Walmsley, Esq.
196 Information supplied by J. F. Walmsley, Esq. and Dennis Johnson, Esq.
197 Information supplied by David Lloyd, Esq., Director of the Royal School of Needlework
198 Information supplied by Dennis Johnson, Esq.
199 Information supplied by J. F. Walmsley, Esq.
200 *See* Chapter II

Chapter VII

1 Minute Book, 26 March 1926
2 *Cash Book, 1884–1924*, 1902
3 *Ibid.*, 1903
4 *Ibid.*, 1908 and 1909
5 *Ibid.*, 1911
6 *Ibid.*, 1912
7 *Ibid.*, 1913
8 *Ibid.*, 1904
9 *Ibid.*, 1906
10 *Ibid.*, 1914
11 *Ibid.*, *passim* 1914–1918
12 *Ibid.*, 1915
13 Minute Book, 11 July 1932
14 Cash Book, 1884–1924, 1918
15 Cash Book Fol. 220, 1907, 1915 Mr. Cresswell; Minute Book, 26 March 1926
16 *Ibid.*
17 *Ibid.* and List of the Court Livery, 1969, p. 35
18 Minute Book, 26 March 1926
19 *Ibid.*
20 *Ibid.*, 11 October 1943 and 44
21 *Ibid.*, 8 July 1935
22 *Ibid.*, 26 March 1926
23 Minute Book, 8 October 1945, 21 January 1946, 8 April 1946
24 Minute Book, 4 July 1955, 6 October 1956
25 Minute Book, 26 March 1926
26 Minute Book, 6 July 1953
27 Minute Book, 26 March 1926, 6 July 1953
28 Minute Book, 6 July 1953
29 Minute Book, 18 October 1926
30 The Craft Exhibition of 1927
31 Minute Book, 11 July 1927

32 The Craft Exhibition of 1927; Minute Book, 7 October 1929
33 The Craft Exhibition of 1927; Minute Book, 11 July 1927
34 *Ibid.*
35 *Ibid.*, 9 October 1933
36 *Ibid.*, 18 October 1926
37 *Ibid.*, 12 April 1926, 18 October 1926
38 Valuation List, Asprey and Birch and Gaydon Ltd.
39 *Ibid.*, and Minute Book, 17 July 1926
40 Minute Book, 12 January 1931
41 *Ibid.*, 9 October 1933
42 *Ibid.*, 6 April 1936
43 *Ibid.*, 11 April 1932
44 *Ibid.*, 10 April 1933
45 *Ibid.*, 15 October 1928
46 *Ibid.*, 9 January 1939
47 *Ibid.*, 15 October 1928
48 *Ibid.*, 13 October 1930
49 *Ibid.*, 10 October 1932
50 *Ibid.*, 7 October 1935
51 *Ibid.*, 6 January 1936
52 *Ibid.*, 12 October 1936
53 *Ibid.*, 12 October 1931
54 *Ibid.*, 9 October 1933
55 *Ibid.*, 11 October 1937
56 *Ibid.*, 14 April 1930
57 List of the Court and Livery, 1969
58 *Ibid.*
59 Minute Book, 8 July 1935
60 *Ibid.*, 3 April 1939
61 The Craft Exhibition of 1927
62 Minute Book, 11 April 1932
63 *Ibid.*, 4 January 1937
64 *Ibid.*, 3 July 1939
65 *Ibid.*, 8 July 1935
66 *Ibid.*, 13 April 1931
67 *Ibid.*, 11 July 1932
68 *Ibid.*, 4 April 1938, 4 July 1938
69 *Ibid.*, 11 July 1932
70 *Ibid.*, 13 October 1930
71 *Ibid.*, 4 January 1937, 5 April 1937
72 *Ibid.*, 13 July 1931
73 *Ibid.*, 12 October 1931
74 *Ibid.*, 9 January 1933
75 *Ibid.*, 13 July 1931
76 *Ibid.*, 9 October 1933
77 *Ibid.*, 3 April 1935
78 *Ibid.*, 6 July 1936
79 The Craft Exhibition of 1927

80 Minute Book, 5 April 1937
81 *Ibid.*, 10 April 1933
82 *Ibid.*, 4 July 1938
83 *Ibid.*, 3 April 1939
84 *Ibid.*, 9 October 1939
85 *Ibid.*, 8 January 1940
86 *Ibid.*, 9 October 1939
87 *Ibid.*, 6 October 1941
88 *Ibid.*, 5 April 1943
89 *Ibid.*, 6 January 1941
90 *Ibid.*, 7 July 1941
91 The Guildhall Library
92 Minute Book, 9 April 1956
93 Minute Book, 7 April 1941
94 *Ibid.*, 7 July 1941
95 *Ibid.*, 4 January 1943
96 *Ibid.*, 3 April 1944
97 Minute Book, 9 April 1946
98 Minute Book, 6 January 1941
99 Cash Book, 1924
100 Minute Book, 7 July 1941
101 *Ibid.*, 6 October 1941, 4 January 1943, 5 July 1943
102 *Ibid.*, 9 October 1944
103 *Ibid.*, 9 October 1939
104 *Ibid.*, 8 January 1940, 8 July 1940
105 *Ibid.*, 8 July 1940
106 *Ibid.*, 7 October 1940
107 *Ibid.*
108 Minute Book, 13 April 1953
109 *Ibid.*, 6 April 1959
110 Minute Book, 11 October 1943
111 *Ibid.*, 10 January 1944
112 *Ibid.*, 12 October 1942
113 Minute Book, 7 April 1952
114 *Ibid.*, 13 April 1953
115 *Ibid.*, 8 October 1945
116 *Ibid.*, 2 July 1945
117 *Ibid.*, 21 January 1946
118 *Ibid.*, 7 October 1946
119 *Ibid.*, 7 July 1947
120 *Ibid.*, 12 April 1948
121 Minute Book, 10 January 1944
122 Minute Book, 4 July 1949
123 Reports to the Livery
124 Minute Book, 8 July 1946
125 *Ibid.*, 7 July 1952
126 *Ibid.*, 3 July 1961
127 *Ibid.*, 2 July 1956, 7 January 1961

128 *Ibid.*, 14 April 1958
129 *Ibid.*, 2 January 1961
130 *Ibid.*, 6 July 1959
131 *Ibid.*, 11 October 1948, 10 January 1949, 11 April 1949
132 *Ibid.*, 10 October 1949 and information supplied by Philip Cresswell, Esq., C.C.
133 *Ibid.*, 7 July 1952
134 *Ibid.*, 13 October 1952
135 *Ibid.*, 4 January 1954
136 Report to the Livery, 1966
137 Minute Book, 7 July 1947
138 *Ibid.*, 14 April 1958
139 *Ibid.*, 13 October 1958
140 *Ibid.*, 3 July 1961
141 *Ibid.*, 13 January 1947
142 *Ibid.*, 2 April 1951
143 *Ibid.*, 12 April 1954, 11 October 1954
144 *Ibid.*, 4 April 1960
145 *Ibid.*, 12 October 1959
146 *Ibid.*, 10 October 1960
147 *Ibid.*, 3 July 1961; information given by Philip Cresswell, December 1976
148 *Ibid.*, 12 October 1959
149 Vintners' Company records, FD/85 and correspondence files. Other information supplied by W. H. Lloyd-Mead, Esq., then Clerk
150 Letter from Robert Horton, Esq., 6 September 1974
151 Letter from A. Colin Cole, Esq., Windsor Herald of Arms, 14 May 1975
152 *Ibid.*, 9 July 1975
153 *Ibid.*, 9 July 1976
154 Livery List, 1969, and Report to the Livery, 1974
155 Report to the Livery, 1967
156 Minute Book, 2 July 1956
157 *Ibid.*, 6 October 1956
158 *Ibid.*, 8 April 1957
159 *Ibid.*, 9 April 1956
160 Report to the Livery, 1974
161 Reports to the Livery, 1972–74
162 Minute Book, 8 October 1945
163 *Ibid.*, 7 July 1958
164 *Ibid.*, 12 January 1948
165 *Ibid.*, 10 October 1949
166 *Ibid.*, 2 April 1962
167 Report to the Livery, 1966
168 Livery List, 1969
169 Minute Book, 14 April 1958
170 *Ibid.*, 4 April 1960
171 Report to the Livery, 1966
172 *Ibid.*, 1967/8
173 *Ibid.*, 1968/9
174 *Ibid.*, 1969/70

175 *Ibid.*, 1972
176 *Ibid.*, 1973
177 *Ibid.*, 1974
178 Minute Book, 13 April 1953, 6 July 1953
179 *Ibid.*, 12 October 1953
180 *Ibid.*, 2 April 1962
181 Report to the Livery, 1969/70
182 *Ibid.*, 1966
183 Minute Book, *passim*
184 Letter from Robert Horton, Esq., 6 September 1974
185 Report to the Livery, 1974
186 Livery List, 1969
187 Minute Book, 7 October 1940
188 Report to the Livery, 1967/8
189 Minute Book, 12 April 1954
190 *Ibid.*, 9 April 1956
191 Report to the Livery, 1972
192 Minute Book, 10 January 1944
193 Report to the Livery, 1969/70
194 *Ibid.*, 1972
195 *Ibid.*, 1972 and 1973
196 *Ibid.*, 1974
197 Clerk's letter to the Livery, 4 July 1974
198 Minute Book, 10 April 1961
199 Report to the Livery, 1974
200 Minute Book, 8 January 1951 *et passim*
201 *Ibid.*, 7 July 1958
202 *Ibid.*, 3 January 1955, 4 April 1955
203 Report to the Livery, 1972
204 *Ibid.*, 1973
205 *Ibid.*, 1974
206 *Ibid.*, 1967/8
207 Minute Book, 3 July 1961
208 Report to the Livery, 1968/9
209 Minute Book, 13 January 1947, 7 January 1957 *et passim*

List of the Masters of the Company

FROM THE INCORPORATION OF THE COMPANY TO DATE

1693/4	Nathaniel Smith.	1742	Robert Pitter.
1695	Thomas Wright.	1743	Nicholas Cunliffe.
1696	Thomas Bracee.	1744	Robert Glyde.
1697	Daniel Biddle.	1745	Thomas Gardiner.
1698/9	Robert Rhodes.	1746	John Embry.
1700	Daniel Field.	1747/8	Benjamin Lane.
1701/2	Christopher Blower.	1749	William Jephcote.
1703	Henry Southouse.	1750	Robert Crew.
1704	Francis Greene.	1751	Samuel Crouch.
1705	Thomas Price.	1752	John Walklate.
1706	John Shayler.	1753	Andrew Aylesbury.
1707	Edward Page.	1754/5	John Court.
1708	Richard Andrew.	1756	Daniel How.
1709	John Lane.	1757	William Read.
1710/11	Charles Hosier.	1758	John Waller.
1712	John French.	1759	Samuel Plumb.
1713/4	Walter Turner.	1760/1	George Vaughan.
1715/6	Joseph Tucker.	1762	Hewson Scott.
1717	Richard Taylor.	1763	Edmund Tanner.
1718/9	George Prestland.	1764	John Macartney.
1720/1	William Southouse.	1765	Joseph Atkinson.
1722/3	Pauncefort Green.	1766	Stephen Crouch.
1724/5	William Harker.	1767	William Dracutt.
1726/7	Walter Crew.	1768	Benjamin Goffe.
1728/9	Godwin Washbourne.	1769	Henry Questead.
1730/3	Daniel Mallory.	1770	George Naylor.
1733	Lionel Barnes (died Samuel Morris successor).	1771	Thomas Brown.
		1772	Thomas Dewin.
1734/5	Richard Drury.	1773	Benjamin Dewin.
1736/7	John Haynes.	1774	William Stackhouse.
1738	John Dodsworth.	1775	Adam Bellinger.
1739	Edmund Tanner.	1776	Richard Sturley.
1740	Richard Cook.	1777	Samuel Roberts.
1741	Robert Berkeley.	1778	John Studdard.

Year	Name	Year	Name
1779	William Turner.	1833	William Walker.
1780	John Read.	1834	John Atherley.
1781	Thomas Taunton.	1835	Henry Johnson Appleford.
1782	William Gomme.	1836	Edward Stillwell.
1783	Joseph Carter.	1837	James Boys.
1784	Joseph Allen.	1838	James Botson McClary.
1785	Charles Scott.	1839	George Scovell.
1786	John Scarnell.	1840	Henry Wm. Johnson.
1787	John Miles.	1841	William Bullmore.
1788	Charles Lockwood.	1842	Thomas Hackett.
1789	Thomas Boys.	1843	Michael Solomon.
1790	William K. Wigginton.	1844	Ferdinand F. Camroux.
1791	William Stackhouse.	1845	Alfred A. McClary.
1792	John Richardson.	1846	Henry Bland.
1793	Richard Lowther.	1847	John Lane.
1794	Richard Birch.	1848	Samuel McClary.
1795	Samuel Fearne.	1849	William Burgin.
1796	Edward Hale.	1850	Thomas Burgin, Junr.
1797	Edward Utton.	1851	John Burgin.
1798	John Proudley.	1852	Benjamin White.
1799	John Chupcey.	1853	Owen Clutton.
1800	Edward Mottrom.	1854/5	Frederick J. Campbell.
1801	William Turner, Junr.	1856	Richard M. Miles.
1802	Thomas Chapman.	1857/8	Edward S. Stillwell.
1803	William Reeves.	1859	James R. Reynolds.
1804	Henry Turner.	1860	George Benton.
1805	James Norton.	1861	George Simons.
1806	John Uffington.	1862	William Clayton.
1807/8	John Mills.	1863	Charles F. Corney.
1809	Richard Lowther.	1864	Edwin Newell.
1810	Joseph Fearne.	1865/6	Charles Gammon.
1811	Lewis Miles.	1867	John W. Marshall.
1812/4	Joseph Turner.	1868	George O. Camroux.
1815/8	Thomas Boys, Junr.	1869	William Mashman.
1819	Robert Reynolds.	1870	Frederick Stanton.
1820	William James.	1871	David Henry Jacobs.
1821	Joseph Johnson.	1872	Edward Burke.
1822	John Fearne.	1873	Henry William Johnson.
1823	James Scovell.	1874	George Foster.
1824	Samuel McClary.	1875	J. G. Johnson.
1825	Nicholas Boys.	1876/7	Francis Pendered.
1826	Joseph Fearne.	1878/9	George Davenport.
1827	William Lewis.	1880	John K. Luck.
1828	Bilcliffe Martin.	1881	Thomas Gerrard Fletcher.
1829	James Reynolds.	1882/3	George Kenning.
1830	Thomas Burgin.	1884/6	Major Hymen A. Joseph, C.C.
1831	Ferdinand R. Camroux.	1887	James Knapton Abel.
1832	James Scovell.	1888	Horace Stewart.

1889/91	Gabriel Lindo, C.C., F.R.G.S.	1937	Lt.-Col. H. P. L. Cart de Lafontaine, O.B.E., T.D., F.R.I.B.A.
1892/3	William Hays.		
1894	Edmond Frank Brewster Fuller.	1938	Colonel Norman L. Ball, J.P.
1895/7	Lt.-Col. Phineas Cowan.	1939	C. Digby Stillwell.
1898	James Bishop.	1940	C. Digby Stillwell.
1899	Benjamin Louis Cohen, M.P.	1941	James H. Morton, F.C.A., C.C.
1900	Col. Sir J. Roper Parkington, J.P., D.L.	1942	Roland G. Benton.
		1943	Alderman Sir George Wilkinson, Bart.
1901	Matthew Righton Webb, J.P., F.S.A.	1944	John L. Cridlan, A.M.I.C.E., A.M.I.Mech.E.
1902/3	Edward Lee, C.C.	1945	Harold G. C. Fairweather.
1904	Alfred J. Hollington, J.P.	1946	Wilfred W. Nops, LL.B.
1905	Thomas Blair.	1947	Alderman Sir Frederick Tidbury-Beer.
1906	William Shurmuir, J.P.	1948	William C. Brett, C.C.
1907	Sir Richard Stapley, J.P., C.C.	1949	Leslie W. Johnson.
1908	Edwin Fox.	1950	Edgar Wheeler, C.C.
1909	Major Sir Harry North, J.P., D.L.	1951	Alderman Sir Denys C. F. Lowson, Bart., M.A.
1910	James Speller.		
1911	Sir Thomas H. Brooke-Hitching.	1952	Howard G. Hicklenton.
1912	Jas. S. Crowther, J.P.	1953	Frank W. Guttridge, I.S.O.
1913	Cuthbert Wilkinson, L.C.C.	1954	Hubert A. Gill, C.M.G., M.A.
1914	Col. and Alderman Sir William H. Dunn, Bart.	1955	Leonard Bingham.
		1956	Ernest W. Watts, F.C.A., C.C.
1915	Alfred Charles Latter.	1957	Ernest H. Fairbairn.
1916	Robert Arkley Cuthbertson.	1958	L. Murray Johnson.
1917	David Haes.	1959	Benjamin G. Arthur, C.B.E., C.C.
1918	William A. C. Norwood.	1960	James W. Perry.
1919	Albert E. L. Slazenger, C.C.	1961	Herbert G. D. Toye.
1920	Sir Harry S. Foster, J.P., D.L.	1962	Frederick A. Grant, J.P.
1921	Commendatore Enrico Arbib.	1963	George E. Baker.
1922	Sir Harry F. Hepburn, C.C.	1964	Dennis H. L. Johnson.
1923	R. Stafford Charles, F.S.I.	1965	Albert S. Gregg.
1924	H. T. Cart de Lafontaine, M.A.	1966	Bernard Thorpe.
1925	W. J. Trice, C.C.	1967	Philip H. Cresswell, C.C.
1926	Alderman Sir Maurice Jenks, Bart., LL.D., F.C.A.	1968	George K. Perkins, F.A.I.
		1969	Leslie Balfour Boyd.
1927	Fred Gillett, C.C.	1970	Frank Osbaldston Murgan Smith.
1928	A. Rochester Brown.	1971	Andrew Gurney Johnson, F.C.A.
1929	R. H. Hedderwick.	1972	Clifford William Jeapes.
1930	A. Stanley Bell, C.C.	1973	Douglas Francis Dunstan, F.C.I.I.
1931	Alderman Sir Harold G. Downer, LL.B.	1974	Robert George Chandler Horton, F.C.A.
1932	Colonel Stephen Simpson, N.A., T.D., D.L.	1975	Leslie Robert Spencer Cork.
		1976	Ronald Arthur Ralph Hedderwick, C.C.
1933	A. E. Watts, F.C.A., C.C.		
1934	Charles S. Syrett.	1977	G. H. Ross Goobey, F.I.A.
1935	Sir Henry Curtis-Bennett, K.C.	1978	R. C. A. FitzGerald, M.A.
1936	Arthur W. Jarratt.		

Clerks of the Company

1694	John Borrett (the City Solicitor).	1820	Richard S. Taylor.
1702	William Borrett.	1822	Jacob Mould.
1714	William Hilditch.	1824	Samuel Lepard.
1718	Samuel Briggs.	1865	Charles Gammon.
1721	Andrew Osborne.	1891	Wynne E. Baxter, J.P., D.L.
1739	Nathaniel Stable and Joseph Brian.	1919	A. Charles Knight, J.P., F.S.A., C.C.
1740	Jasper Bull.	1955	Philip H. Cresswell, C.C.
1748	Thomas Harris.	1967	Norman H. Harding.
1774	Joseph Ducker.	1968	*Philip H. Cresswell, C.C.
1778	William Robins.	1974	David Reid, F.C.A.

Beadles

1694	Richard Brady.	1826	John Burgin.
1701	George Meakins.	1856	George Burgin.
1723	John Leech.	1866	Abraham Hervey.
1736	Richard Drury.	1880	[Blank] Lovell.
1743	Robert Wrathall.	1931	[Blank] Rawles.
1767	James Dennis.	1956	Reginald A. Baldock.
1796	William King Wiggington.	1976	H. F. Moore.
1810	Richard Pugh.		

Index

Abell, Mathew: 28
Abott, Mathew: 28
Abrahams, Marcus: 34
Academy, the Royal: 52; Burlington House, 59
Accrington: 44
Adolphus Frederick, Prince: 40
Albert, Prince Consort: 31
Alice H.R.H. Princess, Countess of Athlone: 62
Amsterdam: 24
Anderson, Sir Colin F.R.S.A., Provost of the R.C.A.: 62
Art, Royal College of: 62; Provost's Gown of, 62
Andrews, Richard: 13
Antiquaries, Society of: 5
Apuleius: 1
Arms, College of: 28, 29; Court of Chivalry of, 29, 35
Arts, the Royal Society of: 52
Arthur, Prince of Connaught Golf Competition: 56
Arundel: 40
Ashburnham, Lord: 40
Attorney General, the: 13, 14, 15, 18
Augsburg: 1
Augustus Frederick, Prince: 40
Australia: 48, 49; Commonwealth Stock, 55
Avenham Road, No. 42, Preston, Lancs.: 45
Aytom, James: 23

Babington, Richard: 1, 8
Bahrein: 49
Bailey's: 42
Baker, George F.: 57
Balaclava, Battle of: 31
Baldock, Mr.: 58
Ball, Norman L., J. P.: 52, 54
Baltic Exchange, the: 59

Barde, Francis de: 6
Barnes, John: 46
Barnet: 53, 57
Barnsbury: 50
Barret and Corney (Cornie): 32, 39, 40–41, 44, 46
Barret, Bryan: 39
Barret, Bryan the Younger: 39
Barret, John: 39
Barry's: 42
Barton, George: 39, 44
Bath, Assembly Rooms at: 23
Baverstock, Thomas John: 42
Baxter, Wynne E., J.P., D.L.: 37
Bede: 5
Bedford, Earl of: 8, 11; William, Son of, 11
Bedfordshire: 45
Belfast: 44
Belfast, H.M.S.: 59
Bell, A. Stanley, C.C.: 52, 57
Bennet, Sir Henry Curtis, K.C.: 52
Bennet, Samuel: 18
Benson, Thomas: 16
Bentham, Jeremiah: 40
Benton and Johnson: 36, 39, 42, 44, 46, 47, 48, 49
Benton, George: 36, 41, 47, 48, 52; See also Gold and Silver Wire Drawing Firms
Benton, Roland: 39, 41, 42, 44, 61; See also Gold and Silver Wire Drawing Firms
Benton, Mrs.: 47, 48
Bernays, Albert: 57
Berry, William: 28
Berwick on Tweed: 19
Bevan, Mr.: 23
Biddle, Daniel: 13
Bindoff, S. T.: 9
Bingham, L.: 60
Blackburn: 44
Blower, Christopher: 13, 28

Boast, Isabella Ellen: 45, 46
Boleyn, Queen Anne, Consort of Henry VIII: 6
Bonnixi, Lawrence: 6
Borrett and Borney, See Gold and Silver Wire Drawing Firm Barrett and Corney
Borrett, John: 13, 17, 19, 29, 51
Borrett, William: 19
Boyd, General, Officers of: 40
Boyd, Leslie: 57, 59, 61
Bracee, Thomas: 13
Bradbourn, Master: 11
Bradford, Samuel: 25
Brady, Richard: 19
Bridewell, The Art Masters of: 2 30
Brighton: 40
Bromley (Kent), Parish Clerk of: 11
Brown, Joseph: 25, 29
Brown, Rochester: 52
Bruce, John: 23
Buck A. E., The Elder: 46
Buck A. E., The Younger: 46
Buckinghamshire: 45, 46
Bull, Charles: 26
Burchall, Edward: 7
Burford, Rose de: 5
Burlington House, See Academy Royal
Burnett, Mr.: 29

Camroux, Ferdinand Richard: 3 38
Camroux, John Lewis: 22, 26
Canada: 48, 49
Canterbury: 40
Cardigan, Earl of: 31
Carlisle, Lord: 11
Cassells, J. D.: 52
Cave, Thomas: 37
Chadderton, Bertha: 47

86

Chadderton, William: 47
Chancellor, the Lord: 17
Channon, Lt. Commander: 61
Chaponier, Ann: 41
Charles I: 8, 10, 15
Charles II: 11, 15
Charlotte, Queen, Consort of George III: 31, 40
Chatalan, M.: 24
Cheshire, John: 16
China: 23, 38, 43
Cistercians, the: 5
Clayton, William: 25
Coke, Sir Edward: 10
Cold Bath Square Prison: 44
Cole, A. Colin: 58
Cole, Harold: 57
Cole, Mrs.: 57
Coles, Martha: 53
Collins, Thomas: 26
Common Pleas, the Lord Chief Justice of: 17
Commonwealth Trading Week Exhibition: 61
Conway, General: 40
Copper Wire: 1; Copper Wire Drawers, 17
Cordingley, Mr.: 33
Corney, Charles F.: 41; *See also* Gold and Silver Wire Drawing Firms
Corney, J. B.: 36, 39; *See also* Gold and Silver Wire Drawing Firms
Corney, Thomas: 39
Court, John: 28
Cousens, William: 13
Coventry, The Mayor and Bailiffs of: 24, 25; Trade in, 24, 25, 32, 42, 43, 44
Cowper, The Earl: 40
Cresswell, Philip H., C.C.: 57, 58, 59
Cromwell, Oliver, the Lord Protector: 11
Croom, Richard: 16
Cumberland, The Duke of, Prince Ernest Augustus: 40
Cunliffe, Nicholas: 28
Customs, Commissioners of: 23
Customs House, the: 23
Cuthbert, Saint: 5
Cuthbertson, Robert: 52
Czar, the: 8

Danner's, Konrad: 45
Darcy, Alison: 5

Darley, Robert: 17
Darwen: 44
Davers, Sir Robert: 18
Davies, James: 39
Davies, Mr.: 39
D'Avigdor, Miss Estelle: 36
Day, John: 16
Defence, Ministry of: 49
De Keyser, Lady: 35
De Keyser, Sir Polydore: 34, 35
Dell, Mr: 23
Dennis, James: 33
Dentith, A. W.: 60
Devonshire: 45
Devonshire, The Duke of: 40
Dichon, Thomas Guy: 5
Dickens, Charles: *Barnaby Rudge* by, 27
Doncaster: 40
Douglas, Miss Marie: 36
Downer, Sir Harold, LL.B.: 52
Dragoons, 11th Light: 31
Dron, Lady: 52
Dujardin, Francois: 41
Dunstan, Douglas: 59, 60
Durham, High Sheriff of: 52
Durham, Simeon of: 5

Edward I: 5
Edward VI: 6
Edward VII: 51
Edwards, Miss: 53
Egypt: 48, 54
Elizabeth I: 9
Elizabeth II: 32
Elizabeth of York, Consort of Henry VII: 5
Eloi, Saint: 11
Emaer, Sir John: 57
Embassy, for the French Marriage: 8
England: 48
Essex, the County of: 8
Etherington, Mr.: 42
Europe: 24
Excise, Commissioners of: 1, 24

Farrow, Samuel: 16
Field, Daniel: 13
Field, John: 13
Fielding, Ada: 46
Fielding, Ivy: 46
Firmin, G. V.: 42; *See also* Firmins
Firmin, J. W.: 42; *See also* Firmins
Firmins, Button makers: 42
First Anti-Aircraft Division, R.A.S.C., T.A.: 54

Fisher, John: 13
Fitch, E. C.: 45, 48
Florence: 5, 6
Floyer, Peter: 13
Forest, Mary: 7
Fournier, Anthony: 1
Fowle, Matthias: 10, 14
Fox, Charles James: 31
Framlyngham, Anne: 6
Framlyngham, John: 6
France: 21, 23, 24, 30, 49; Revolution in, 31, 39

Gares, Mr.: 4, 11
Garill, John: 15
Garroway, Alderman Francis: 8, 14, 49
Garrard, Mr.: 39
Gaskell, Elizabeth, *North and South* by, 27, 15
Genoa: 5
George II: 24
George III: 23, 31, 40
George IV: 40
George V: 53
George VI: 55
Gerder, Michael: 57
Germany: 1, 44, 47
Gibbon, Mr.: 24
Gibbs, Alderman: 11
Gieves: 48
Gill, H. A.: 60
Gillet, Fred: 52, 53
Glasgow: 32, 44, 47
Glyde, Mr.: 25
Gold and Silver Lace: 4, 18, 21, 23, 24, 31, 32, 35, 41, 51, 61
Gold and Silver Wire:
  Acts of Parliament About, 4, 18, 19, 24
  Assay of, 8, 10, 11
  Control of by the Company, 13, 15, 17
  Embroidery Using, 5–6, 31, 32
  Engine Spinners in, 16, 22
  Excise of, 1, 24, 34
  Extent of, 16
  Firms Engaged in, *See* Barret and Corney; Benton and Johnson; Johnson's; Kenning's, David; Makinson, E. & W. G.; Sharp's, John; Simpson and Rook; Simpson's, Stephen; Stanton's; Toottell, G. H. L.; Toye Kenning and Spencer Ltd.; Van's
  French in, 22;

87

Hand Spinners in, 7, 22;
Making, 1–3, 6–7;
Masonic Regalia, 40, 42, 48;
Monopolies in, 9–11;
Prices, 9, 41;
Trade in, 5;
Use of Powered Machinery in, 1–3;
Venice making, 6, 7, 8;
Wages of People Involved in, 7, 41, 46;
Women in, 15, 22
Gold and Silver Wyre Drawers Company: *See* London City Livery Companies
Gold, Field of the Cloth of: 6
Gold Lace and Embroiderers' Association: 61
Gordon Riots: 27
Grant, Frederick A., J.P.: 57
Graunger, Josine: 6
Great Exhibition, The, 1851: 34
Great Harwood: 44
Greenwich: 59
Grimshaw, Alexander: 47
Guards, the bandsmen of: 4
Guildhall: *See* London, Corporation of
Gutridge, F. W., I.S.O.: 60

Hall, Thomas: 7
Hanmaker, Mr.: 26
Hanyngton, Christopher: 6
Harding, Norman, C.C.: 33, 57, 58
Hardwick, Lord: 40
Harridge, Samuel: 13
Harris, Job: 13
Harrison, Thomas: 41
Hedderwick, Ralph: 59
Henrietta Maria, Queen, Consort of Charles I: 11, 15
Henry VIII: 6, 8, 9
Hepburn, Mr.: 38
Herodotus: 1
Herrenden, Mr.: 6
Hickcox, Zachary: 13
Hicklenton, Mr.: 54
Hinks, Madame Pemberton: 36
Hobart, Sir Henry, M.P.: 18
Hobson's: 48
Hody, William: 6
Holland: 24
Holmes, Thomas: 41
Hoover, President: 50
Horrocks, Crewdson: 46
Horsley, Joseph: 13

Horsly, John: 18
Horton, Robert: 59, 60, 61
Hotels, Restaurants, Inns etc.: Albion Tavern the, 36; Cannon Street Hotel, the, 36; Connaught Rooms, the, 55; Criterion, Restaurant, the, 36; De Keyser's Hotel, 50; George and Vulture, the, in Cheapside, 29, 33; Globe Tavern, the, near Stocks Market, 25; Half Moon Tavern, in Cheapside, 29; Kings Arms, the, 23; Metropole Hotel, the, 36; Savoy Hotel, the, 59; Thatched House the, P.H., 40
Houblon, Jacob: 31
Household Cavalry, State Trumpeters of: 4
Howard, Sir John: 5
Huguenots: 21
Hungerford, Dame Agnes: 6
Hussars, 11th (P.A.O.), (the Cherry Pickers): 31
Hussars, 14th: 36
Hussey, John: 8
Hutchins, Miss: 42

India: 43, 47, 48, 49
International Health Exhibition 1884, The: 35
Ireland: 41, 48
Isaacs, Asher: 34
Isaacs, Sir Henry Aaron: 34
Isaacs, Lewis: 34
Isaacs, Samuel: 34
Isabella, wife of Edward II: 5
Italy: 22, 24

James I: 9, 10, 14
Japan: 55; Sterling Loan, 55
Javan, John Thomas: 39
Jeapes, Clifford: 59, 60
Jefferies, Joseph: 42
Jenks, Sir Maurice, Bt., LL.D.: 52
Jews: 11, 34
Jett, Thomas: 13
Johnson, Andrew: 42, 57, 61; *See also* Gold and Silver Wire drawing firms
Johnson, Cyril: 48
Johnson, Dennis H. L.: 39, 42, 57, 61; *See also* Gold and Silver Wire drawing firms

Johnson, Henry: 47
Johnson, Henry William: 36, 39, 41, 44, 51
Johnson, Henry William, the third: 47, 48
Johnson, Herbert William: 48
Johnson, Joseph: 41; *See also* Gold and Silver Wire drawing firms
Johnson, Leslie: 42, 47; *See also* Gold and Silver Wire drawing firms
Johnson, Leslie W.: 42, 55; *See also* Gold and Silver Wire drawing firms
Johnson, L. Murray: 42, 61; *See also* Gold and Silver Wire drawing firms
Johnson, Sidney: 47, 48
Johnson's: 42
Joseph, Hymen Aaron, C.C.: 37
Junior Carlton Club: Disraeli Room of, 59

Kennedy, Mr.: 23
Kenning, George: 35, 36, 42; *See also* Gold and Silver Wire drawing firms
Kenning's David: 36, 39, 43
Kent, The Duke of, Prince Edward: 40
Kew William: 23
Kings Bench, Lord Chief Justice of: 13, 17
Knight, Athro Charles, J.P., F.S.A., C.C.: 51, 52, 54, 55, 58
Krupp's: 45
Kaupp, Annie: 46
Kentish-Barnes, Jeremy John, A.C.A.: 47
Kentish-Barnes, William Stephen: 47

Lafontaine, Lt. Col. Cart de: 52, 53, 55, 56
Lancashire, Trade for: 32, 43, 44, 47
Langmead, Lile Arthur: 42
Lazarus, Lewis: 34
Leigh, Edward: 47
Leigh, Edward Howard: 47, 48
Leigh, J. & A.: 46
Leipzig: 24
Lennox, Lady: 40
Lepard, Samuel: 33
Lewisham: 43
Lincoln: 40
Lindo, Gabriel: 38

Lister, Rt. Hon. Sir Philip Cunliffe, M.P.: 52
Liverpool: 40
Lombe, John: 22
London: 5, 27, 39, 50
  Chamberlain of, 8, 20
  Churches;
    St. James Garlickhythe, 60; St. Mary Le Bow, 60; St. Paul's, 50, 60
  City and Guilds Institute, 61
  City Arts Trust Ltd., 60
  City Livery Club, 57
  City Livery Companies, 8, 37; Commissions on, 37
    Apothecaries the Co. of and Hall of, 55
    Armourers the Company of, 17
    Artillery Company the Honourable, 61; Armoury House, 59
    Blacksmiths the Company of, 2, 17
    Broderers the Company of, 5, 7, 8, 17, 62
    Clothworkers the Company of, 17, 62; Hall of, 35, 50
    Cordwainers the Company of, 17
    Drapers the Company of, 62
    Fishmongers the Company of, 17
    Girdlers the Company of, 8
    Glass Sellers the Company of, 15
    Glovers the Company of, 17, 61
    Gold and Silver Wyre Drawers the Company of, 13–30, 32–36, 50–62
      Apprentices, 16, 17, 18, 20, 25, 26, 34
      Arms of, 28, 29, 35, 57–58
      Banners of, 51, 52, 57
      Beadle of, 13, 17, 19, 25, 30, 33, 52, 54, 58
      Byelaws, 17, 18, 26, 27, 29, 30, 33, 34, 62
      Charity, 50, 53, 54, 60
      Charter of Incorporation, 13, 30, 33, 38, 58, 62
      Clerk of, 13, 17, 19, 30, 33, 37, 38, 51, 55, 56, 57, 58, 60; Offices of, 54
      Court of, 13, 20, 21, 55, 56
      Dinners etc., 29, 33, 36, 50, 52, 53, 54, 55, 56, 58, 59, 62
      Hall of, 34, 56
      History written of, 36
      Income and Capital of, 20, 37, 38, 53, 54, 55, 56, 57, 58, 59
      Livery, 17, 29–30, 32, 51, 54, 55, 56, 60, 61, 62
      Masonic Lodge, 56
      Members of, 13; as Aldermen, 34; as Common Councillors, 33, 34; as Lord Mayors, 34, 35, 59; as Sheriffs, 34, 35, 59
      Plate, 28, 33, 38, 52, 54, 57
      Property, 38, 50, 53
      Renter Warden of, 23, 38
      Stewards, 17, 29
      Stuffmakers in, 16
      Women in, 15, 16, 62
      Working Wire-Drawers in, 16
    Goldsmiths the Company of, 7, 14, 15, 17; Assay Master of, 14; Hall of, 61
    Grocers the Company of, 17, 25; Hall of, 52, 55, 59
    Haberdashers the Company of, 17
    Hat Band Makers the Company of, 17
    Innholders the Company of, and Hall of, 54, 55
    Long Bow String Makers the Company of, 17
    Mercers the Company of, 7, 17, 62
    Merchant Taylors the Company of, 17, 62; Hall of, 52
    Needlemakers the Company of, 62; Salters the Company of, 14, 17, 25; Hall of, 52
    Scriveners the Company of, 17
    Stationers Company, the Company of, Hall of, 51
    Tallow Chandlers, the Company of, Hall of, 59
    Vintners the Company of, 8, 14, 16, 17, 21, 25, 57; Gale and Bernays Dinner of, 57
    Weavers the Company of, 17, 24, 25, 62
  City Solicitor of, 13, 19
  Common Council, the, 19; Members of, 33, 34
  Corporation of, The, 8; Guildhall, 34, 35, 59
  Court of Aldermen of, 13, 14, 25, 27, 28, 37, 55, 58–59; Members of, 34
  Festival of the City of, 60
  Homes for the Elderly, 60
  Lord Mayors, 34, 35, 36, 53; Days, 29; Mansion House, 59
  Lord Mayor's Air Relief Fund the, 54
  Lord Mayor's Comforts League the, 54
  Parishes: all Saints Bread Street, 25; Clerkenwell, 39; Cripplegate, the Churchwardens and Overseers of the Poor of St. Giles, 24, 25; Cripplegate, the Churchwardens and Overseers of the Poor of St Luke, 24, 25
  Recorder of, 13
  Sheriffs, 34, 35, 36
  Streets:
    Aldgate, Southwark, 25
    Barnsbury Terrace, 33
    Bishopsgate Street No. 15, 34
    Cheapside, Half Moon Tavern in, 29
    Cheapside, George and Vulture Tavern in, 29, 33
    Clerkenwell Close No. 28, 39
    Cranbourne Alley, Leicester Fields, 22
    Crooked Lane, 7
    Gloucester Street No. 4., 39
    Green Terrace, 39
    Gutter Lane, 15
    Honey Pot Lane, 25
    Milk Street, 25
    Little Britain No's 9 and 10, 39
    Market Street No. 14, 39
    Sandys Street No. 3, Bishopsgate, 34
    Walbrook No. 33, 54
    Warwick Street No. 8 Regent Street, 42
    White Street No's 1, 6, 11, 16, Cutler Street, 34
    Wood Street, 39
  Town Clerk, the Office of, Clerks in, 30
  Wards: Cripplegate, 25; Moorfields, 25; Vintry the, 25
Lovelace, Henry: 13
Low Mr.: 23
Lowson, Sir Denys: 59
Lucca: 5, 6
Ludgate Gaol: 26
Lycett, Francis: 23
Lyons: 47, 49

Lyons J. & Company: 50

Makinson, E. & W. G.: 47, 48
Malta: 49
Manchester: 41, 47
Mansfield: 45
Mansion House *See* London, Lord Mayors
Marnhull, Orphrey the: 5
Marquerier, Lewis: 22
Marr, the Countess of: 23
Mary, Queen, Consort of George V: 51, 55
Master of the Horse: 40
Mauduitt, Peers: 28
Mecklenburg, Prince Charles of: 40
Melling, Mary *See* Sutton
Mermaid Theatre: 59
Miflin, Richard: 26
Miflin, Mrs.: 26
Military, The Royal Exhibition 1890: 35
Milton, John: 11
Mint, the Assay Master of: 11, 14
Montagu, Duke of *See* Master of the Horse
Montenegrin Red Cross: 50
Montrose, The Duke of: 40
Moore, H. F.: 58
Mortlake: 53
Morton, J. H.: 55
Mount Pleasant P.O., the: 44
Muscovy Company, the: 8
Mytton, Mrs.: 40
Mytton, Squire: 40

Nantes, Revocation of the Edict of: 21, 24
Navy, the Merchant: 4
Navy, the Royal: 4
Needlework, Royal School of (Earlier the School of Embroidery): 1, 42, 49, 62
Nevall, Geoffrey: 52
Newbery, William: 13
Newton, Mr.: 18
New Zealand: 49
New Zealand House, Martini Terrace of: 59
Nigeria: 49
Northamptonshire: 46
Northern Ireland: 32, 44
Nuremberg: 1

Old Bailey, Central Criminal Court: 59

Olympus, H.M.S.: 61
Oporto: 41
Opus Anglicanum: 5
Osborne, John: 20
Oxfordshire: 46

Pakistan: 48, 49
Palmer, C. W.: 54
Parkington, Lady: 50
Parliament: 14, 18, 27, 32, 34
  Acts of:
    Patents Act, 3; 2 Richard II, 5; 25 Henry VII, 17
    Acts re Gold & Silver Wire, 18, 19, 24, 32; re Factories, 46
  Parliament, Attitude of towards Monopolies, 9–10;
  Bills against wearing Gold and Silver lace, 21, 24–25; Lords, House of, 59; Oyer and Terminer, Commissions of, 6, 9
Parratt, Samuel: 13
Pendleton, J.: 41
Pensome, Thomas: 16
Perkins, George: 59
Perry, J. W.: 57
Petre, The Honourable George: 40
Petre, Sir John: 6, 7, 8, 40
Petre, Katherine, Lady: 6
Pitcher, Mr.: 27–28, 30, 32
Potter, William Ely: 42
Preston (Lancs.): 32, 36, 42, 43, 44, 46, 47
Preston, Daniel: 46
Preston, Fred: 46
Preston, Henry: 46
Privy Council, the: 10, 14
Privy Purse, the: 10

Rawles, Mr.: 58
Red Cross, the: 54
Redman, Albert: 1, 48
Rees, Messrs.: 53
Reid, David, F.C.A.: 58
Remonstrance, the Grand: 9
Reynolds, Mr.: 33
Rhodes, Robert: 13
Richards, James: 41
Richmond, The Duke of: 40
Rider, William: 43
Riley, Martha: 45, 46
Ring and Brymer: 50
Rivers, George: 25
Robins, William: 33
Rochester Brown, A.: 52

Rockingham: 40
Rook, Christopher: 36, 41; *See also* Gold and Silver Wire drawing firms Simpson & Rook
Rooke, Miss: 53
Rosineall, John: 7
Ross-Goobey, G.: 57
Royal Exchange, the: 25
Royal Society, the: 24
Russell, Mrs. Christian: 28, 33, 53
Rouse, Robert: 13
Russia: 8, 14, 49

St. John's War Organisation, the: 54
Salisbury: 40
Sandys, Sir Thomas: 8
Saxony: 24
Scatcliffe, Henry: 13
Scotland: 48
Scovell, George: 41; *See also* Gold and Silver Wire drawing firms
Scovell, James: 41; *See also* Gold and Silver Wire drawing firms
Scovell, Mr.: 38, 39, 44
Sendell, George Ernest: 52, 53
Shakespeare, William: 11
Sharp, John: 42; *See also* Gold and Silver Wire drawing firms
Sharp's John: 42, 43, 44, 45, 46, 47, 48
Sheldrake, Jacob: 13
Shrewsbury: 40
Shutz, Mr.: 23
Simmond's: 42
Simpson and Rook: 36, 39, 41, 42
Simpson, Miss Beatrice: 42; *See also* Gold and Silver Wire drawing firms
Simpson, Miss Helen: 42; *See also* Gold and Silver Wire drawing firms
Simpson, Isaac: 3, 39, 41, 44, 45, 46, 47; *See also* Gold and Silver Wire drawing firms
Simpson, Isaac the Younger: 45
Simpson, Stephen (of Mansfield): 45
Simpson, Colonel Stephen, M.A., T.D.: 36, 51, 52; *See also* Gold and Silver Wire drawing firms
Simpson, Stephen the Elder: 42, 45, 47; *See also* Gold and Silver Wire drawing firms
Simpson Stephen: Firm of Stephen Simpson (Est. 1829)

Ltd., 2–4, 6, 39, 42, 43, 44, 45, 46, 47, 48, 49, 61; Works at Preston, 2–4, 42, 43, 44, 45, 46
Sion College *See* London, City Livery Club
Smart, John: 16
Smartfoot, Francis: 13
Smith, A. W.: 52
Smith, Frank, O.M.: 59, 61
Smith, Frederick William: 42
Smith, Nathaniel: 13
Smith, Rebecca: 22
Smith, Samuel: 16
Smith, Mr.: 23
Solomon, Michael: 32, 34
South Africa: 49
Southend: 53
Southouse, Henry: 13
Spanish Succession, War of: 21
Sparrow, Mr.: 14
Spenser, Edmund: 11
Stafford, The Marquis of: 40
Stamford: 40
Stanton, Frederick: 42; *See also* Gold and Silver Wire drawing firms
Stanton, Edwin Alfred: 36; *See also* Gold and Silver Wire drawing firms
Stanton, Horace Frank: 36; *See also* Gold and Silver Wire drawing firms
Stanton's: 36, 39, 43, 48
Star Chamber, Court of: 14
Steiner, Lt. St. John: 61
Stewart, Horace: 36, 37
Stewart, Mr: 35
Stillwell, C. D.: 52, 54, 61; *See also* Stillwells
Stillwell, E.: 54; *See also* Stillwells
Stillwell, E. S.: 54; *See also* Stillwells
Stillwell, Major Eric William Digby: 54
Stillwell, E. W. D. Mrs.: 54
Stillwells: 48
Stormont, Lord: 31
Stow, John: Survey of London of, 28

Strange, Lord: 24
Strike, Charles: 42, 43
Stuarts, the: 9–11
Stubbes, Philip: 9
Sunday Pictorial, the: 43
Sutton, Mary: 44, 47; *See also* Gold and Silver Wire drawing firms Simpsons
Swedish Sextet, the: 36
Swift, William: 13
Swinton, Earl of, *See* Lister, Sir Philip Cunliffe
Sydenham, Mr.: 24

Tawney, Professor R. H.: 9
Taylor, Mary *See* Sutton
Thorpe, Bernard: 56, 57, 59
Thurston, Mr.: 45
Tibson, Jacob: 41
Tootell, George Leigh: 47
Tootell, G. H. L.: 42, 45, 46, 47, 48, 49
Toye, B. E.: 42; *See also* Toye Kenning and Spencer Ltd.
Toye, Frederick: 42; *See also* Toye Kenning and Spencer Ltd.
Toye, Herbert G. D.: 42, 57, 59, 61, 62; *See also* Toye, Kenning and Spencer Ltd.
Toye, Kenning and Spencer Ltd.: 42, 43, 48, 49
Treasurer, the Lord High: 15, 17
Trentham, Lord: 40
Trice W. J.: 52
Trinity House: 59
Trade, Board of: 52
Tucker, Joseph: 13
Turkey: 23
Turner, Edward: 16
Turner, Joseph: 41; *See also* Gold and Silver Wire drawing firms
Turner, Samuel: 25
Turner, William the Elder: 41; *See also* Gold and Silver Wire drawing firms
Turner, William the Younger: 41; *See also* Gold and Silver Wire drawing firms

Urlin, Simon: 15

Van's (Van Oort and Company and Van and Turner): 39, 41, 44
Vatican, the: 5
Venetians, the: 1
Venice: 5, 6, 7, 8, 24
Vernon, Lord: 40
Victoria R.: 31, 34; Tutor in Hindustani of, 51
Villiers, Sir Edward: 10
Vincent, Sir Percy: 52
Violet, Thomas: 4, 7, 10, 14, 50

Wales: 48
Wales, Prince of, Funds sponsored by: 50, 53
Waller, John: 24
Walker, Mrs.: 52
Walmsley, J. T.: 46, 61
Walton, Jeremiah: 25
Warwick, Sir Philip: 15
Washborne, Philip: 2, 16, 18
Wastfield, William: 13
Watts, A. E., F.C.A.: 52
Watts, E. W., F.C.A.: 60
Westcliffe on Sea: 50
Whitchurch (Glamorgan): 53
White, Miss: 53
Wiggington, William King: 33
Wilhelm II, Kaiser: 51
Wilkes, John: 27
Wilkinson, Sir George, Bt., K.C.V.O.: 56, 59, 60
William III, War of: 21
Williams, Mr.: 22
Windsor Herald *See* Cole, A. Colin
Woods, Thomas: 13
Wright, Miss Ethel: 36
Wright, Thomas: 13
Wydeslade, John: 6

York: 40
York, The Duke of: 40

Zeruga Minstrels, the: 36